SPECTACULAR WASHINGTON

SPECTACULAR
WASHINGTON
VON HARDESTY
BEAUX ARTS EDITIONS

Spectacular Washington

Copyright © 2004 Hugh Lauter Levin Associates, Inc.
ISBN: 0-88363-616-6

Produced by
Charles O. Hyman, Visual Communications, Inc.
Washington, D.C.

Designed by
Kevin Osborn, Research & Design, Ltd.
Arlington, Virginia

Melissa Payne, *Project Editor*
Deborah T. Zindell, *Copyeditor*
Lawrence DiRicco, *Researcher*
Gene Eisman, *Consulting Editor*

Illustrations Credits
Position on page: T = top, B = bottom, C = center, L = left, R = right

MICHAEL GEISSINGER: 6, 25L, 27, 57, 88B.

CAROL HIGHSMITH: 28–29, 36T, 37T, 44L,R, 50T, 52–53, 58, 59T,B, 60–61, 62–63, 66BR, 78–79, 85R, 86–87, 88C, 106B, 106–107, 108L, 108–109, 109R, 122BR, 124–125.

ROBERT C. LAUTMAN: 29, 30R,L, 72 Courtesy of the Chief Architect, GSA, 80T,B, 85L, 100, 101C.

FRED J. MAROON: 1, 17, 20TR, 22L, 25R, 26R, 32, 38–39, 40–41, 42–43, 45, 50B, 55, 56, 58–59, 66L, 67, 68, 77, 81B, 98T, 104–105, 106T, 116–117, 119, 120–121, 122L, 126–127, 128–129, 130–131, 132.

FOLIO, INC. PHOTOGRAPHS: J. Sohm/Panoramic Images 2–3, John Skowronski 4–5, Richard Cummins 7, Vito Palmisano/Panoramic Images 11–13, Jeff Mitchell 14–15, Everett C. Johnson 15T, John W. Keith 15BL, Fred J. Maroon 15BR, Brad Markel 16T, Don Hammerman 16B, Kit Walling 18L, Robert C. Shafer 18TR, Cameron Davidson 19, Matthew Borkoski 20L, Alan Goldstein 21, Paul M. Franklin 22–23, 23, Cameron Davidson 24, Richard T. Nowitz 26L, Robert Llewellyn 28TL, John Skowronski 28BL, Cameron Davidson 31, Neil Meyerhoff/Panoramic Images 33–35, Fred J. Maroon 36B, Skip Brown 37B, Robert C. Shafer 46, Mark Segal 47–49, Michael Ventura 51L, Robert C. Shafer 51BR, Cameron Davidson 54, Michael Ventura 64L, Richard T. Nowitz 64R, Michael Ventura 66TR, Richard Sisk/Panoramic Images 69–71, Mark Segal 73, Richard Cummins 74, Rick Buettner 75T, Michael Anderson 75B, Everett C. Johnson 76, 81T, Patricia Fisher 88L, Joe Jacobson/Panoramic Images 91–93, Greg Pease 94–95, Robert C. Shafer 98B, Lelia G. Hendren 99, 100–101, Yogi Kaufman 101R, John Skowronski 102L, Richard T. Nowitz 102R, 103L, Alan Goldstein 103R, Al Messerschmidt 109L, Vladpans/Panoramic Images, 113–115, Robert C. Shafer 118, Richard Quataert 122TR, Ted Hooper 123, Patricia Fisher 124, Paul M. Franklin, 125.

ADDITIONAL SOURCES: The Library of Congress 9, Eric Long 10, Marc Maroon 51TR, International Spy Museum 65, Dennis Brack 80–81, Eric Long NASM 82L, Caroline Russo NASM 82R, Eric Long NASM 83, Edward Owen USNHM 84, Vietnam Veterans Memorial Collection 88T, Eric Long 89, Paul Morse/ The White House 90, White House Historical Association 95, 96–97, Hillwood Museum and Gardens 104, 105T,B, Jessie Cohen, Smithsonian's National Zoo 110–111, Susan Sterner/The White House 112.

PRINTED IN CHINA

CONTENTS

INTRODUCTION

In June 1791, President George Washington, accompanied by French architect and engineer Pierre Charles L'Enfant, made a survey of a strip of land along the shores of the Potomac River—what later became Washington, D.C. Atop one elevated point, then called Jenkins Hill, they gazed out over a dramatic vista of rolling hills, scattered tobacco farms, and wooded plots. The landscape—if primitive and undeveloped—appeared to both men as the ideal seat or "residence" for the newly established United States of America. For the visionary L'Enfant, Jenkins Hill offered a "pedestal waiting for a monument"—and he dreamed of a metropolis of sublime beauty and grandeur, a capital city that would one day rival Paris and London.

Spectacular Washington captures this visionary city of L'Enfant's dreams, as it now appears at the turn of the twenty-first century. Today Washington, D.C., mirrors the essential thrust of L'Enfant's plan to transform "a wilderness into a city." The nation's capital is a city characterized by openness and magnificent vistas. Broad radiating avenues, linked to a series of focal points or circles, give expression to a blueprint—a blueprint always subject to alteration and refinement. The

Mall, with its grandiose sweep from Capitol Hill to the Potomac River, is a national park of unique beauty, lined with public buildings, museums, art galleries, and war memorials.

Spectacular Washington provides a lively visual perspective, casting light on the nation's capital through more than one prism—the Potomac River, Georgetown, Downtown, the Mall, the Avenues, and Capitol Hill. In and around the brick, limestone, and granite structures that give definition to Washington, D.C., there is also a mood, something intangible, a pervading sense that the city is a living symbol of American democracy—the embodiment of the past, the present, and the future of the United States of America.

Building the "Federal City" could be viewed as the culminating moment of the American Revolution. The opening salvo of the Revolution, The Declaration of Independence, in 1776 reflected a powerful yearning to establish a new and self-governing nation, not merely colonial resentment toward taxes and the usurpation of the British Parliament's political power. Over the next quarter century, there were many historical milestones: a successful seven-year war of independence; the writing of the Constitution

THE U.S. CAPITOL.
The Capitol dome offers a dramatic backdrop for a cluster of rising balloons.

THE ANDREW JACKSON STATUE.
The equestrian statue of President Andrew Jackson, sculpted by Clark Mill, in Lafayette Square. Henry James described the Jackson statue as "the most prodigious of presidential effigies . . . prancing and rocking through the ages."

and the Bill of Rights; the election of George Washington as the first president; and, finally, the establishment of the new government along the Potomac River. The joint session of Congress, meeting for the first time on Jenkins Hill in 1800, represented a moment of climactic triumph in the long struggle for nationhood.

On January 24, 1791, George Washington announced as the permanent location for the new capital a 10-mile stretch of territory at the confluence of the Potomac and Eastern Branch rivers. This decision confirmed the provisions of the Residence Act, passed by Congress the previous year. Andrew Elliott and a free black, Benjamin Banneker, joined the grand enterprise as surveyors. Banneker, a self-educated man with a keen interest in astronomy, laid out boundary stones at one-mile intervals, based on his own celestial calculations. This diamond-shaped tract of land is what we now know as the District of Columbia.

President Washington worked with his secretary of state, Thomas Jefferson, and three commissioners to oversee the initial task of building the first wing of the Capitol, the legislative house for Congress. Jefferson was a

creative force at Washington's side, expressing his own preference for classical architectural styles. Jefferson was an architect in his own right, having designed his Monticello home on the model of an ancient classical temple.

Today, it is difficult to comprehend the rustic nature of Washington, D.C., in 1800, at the time Congress moved into its partially completed structure. The location chosen for the Federal City was challenging to all with its sweltering summer heat, wretched winters, impassable dirt roadways, mosquitoes, and total lack of amenities. The new city consisted of shacks, stretches of tree stumps, and swampland. There were a small number of rough-hewn stores, a few boarding houses, a hotel, and another new government building, the Treasury, located in somber isolation at the west end of the Mall. There were farms on the outskirts, mostly dedicated to the planting of the tobacco crop, still a major source of revenue for the few inhabitants of the District of Columbia. On Capitol Hill, members of Congress found the silence of the primitive environment around them oppressive, a silence broken only by the gunfire of hunters shooting turkeys. But the nation's capital survived its rustic origins to

EARLY PLAN OF THE FEDERAL CITY. *A copy of the 1792 plan for the Federal City by Pierre L'Enfant, reproduced in 1887 by the United States Coastal and Geodetic Survey.*

become a cosmopolitan city and a fitting symbol of the national aspirations of the Founding Fathers.

How Washington developed over two centuries is a long story, reflecting historical circumstance and the architectural whims of the passing generations. There has been a peculiar rhythm to this evolution in urban planning, one best described as eras of building and renovation, alternating with interludes of neglect. L'Enfant, however, articulated the animating principle that would shape the future development of Washington; in his words, "the plan should be drawn on such a scale as to leave room for that aggrandizement and embellishment, which the increase of the wealth of the nation will permit it to pursue at any period however remote." Each generation then received the mandate to build, to engage in the on-going architectural elaboration of the capital.

The notion of Washington as a living city persists into the twenty-first century, as evident in some of the most recent additions to the Mall: the World War II Veterans Memorial and the Smithsonian Institution's National Museum of the American Indian. Building the Federal City is

a relentless endeavor, never to be interrupted even in times of war and national emergency: Abraham Lincoln, for example, approved continuation of the construction work on the new dome of the Capitol while a bloody Civil War raged. The McMillan commission at the turn of the twentieth century led the momentous effort to refashion the Mall into one of the most splendid public spaces on Earth. In more recent times, though, each plan for renewal or proposed additions to Washington's ensemble of national monuments and public buildings must be weighed against competing priorities—and the fact that space is now at a premium. Like the Founding Fathers, Americans still engage in spirited debate over the shape and character of Washington, knowing full well the powerful symbolism associated with the civic architecture of the nation's capital.

Like St. Petersburg, Russia, the other great planned city of the eighteenth century, Washington is still young when compared to ancient capitals such as Rome, London, or Paris. Both Washington and St. Petersburg have stressed the importance of architectural beauty, vast public spaces, and the optimal use of reclaimed

marshland for urban development. The central role of the Potomac parallels the pivotal role of the Neva River in its Russian counterpart. Washington—as with St. Petersburg—offers a pre-modern skyline devoid of the towering presence of skyscrapers.

Whatever parallels may exist with St. Petersburg and other capitals of the world, or whatever homage is owed to the architecture of past civilizations, Washington is an American city—in design, mood, and public uses. We see it in the openness of the city plan, the expansive parks, the moving memorials to past leaders and veterans, and the cultural treasures preserved in its museums. With its commanding place in the geography of Washington, the Capitol possesses special meaning; in the words of Thomas Jefferson, it is "the first temple dedicated to the sovereignty of the people, embellishing with Athenian taste the course of a nation looking far beyond the range of Athenian destinies."

Washington's most famous thoroughfare, Pennsylvania Avenue, reflects the changing character of political life in the twenty-first century. The rise of terrorism in the 1990s brought in its wake some unanticipated and unwelcome changes:

the section of Pennsylvania Avenue dividing the White House from Lafayette Square was closed in 1995. The subsequent terrorist assault on the Pentagon on September 11, 2001, only stiffened the resolve of the federal government to provide security for public buildings and cultural institutions in Washington. Retractable street barriers, uniformed guards, X-ray scanning machines, concrete Jersey barriers doubling as flower pots, and covert high-tech security systems are now—and for the foreseeable future—a normal part of life in the capital. Not since the American Civil War has Washington, D.C., faced the dilemma of providing for public safety even while preserving the ideal of a free and open city.

Still, the values of an open and democratic society define Washington, even in a context of heightened security concerns. When Congress broke ground for its new Visitors Center in 2000, a three-level, underground facility occupying five acres, the Architect of the Capitol sought out a design that would assure "an atmosphere of free and open access." This respect for the values of a democratic society continues to shape the character of the nation's capital in the twenty-first century.

THE RIVER

*"I beheld the course of a large river
abruptly obstructed by rocks, over which it
was breaking with a tremendous roar;
while the foam of the water seemed
ascending to the clouds."*

— JOHN DAVIS OF SALISBURY, 1801

PLAN of the CITY intended for the Permanent SEAT of the Government of the UNITED STATES
Projected agreeable to the direction of the PRESIDENT of the UNITED STATES
OBSERVATIONS explanatory of the PLAN.
Breadth of the Streets.
GEORGE TOWN.
POTOWMAC RIVER.
EASTERN BRANCH.
PART OF VIRGINIA, WITHIN THE FEDERAL DISTRICT.
PART OF MARYLAND, WITHIN THE FEDERAL DISTRICT.
REFERENCES.
References.
Lat. Congress House, ... 38. 53. N.
Long. ...... 0. 0.
SCALE OF POLES.
No 30352 PRICE 50 CENTS
UNITED STATES COAST AND GEODETIC SURVEY OFFICE,
Washington, May 20, 1887.

THE POTOMAC RIVER.
The surging rapids of the Potomac River at Great Falls, Virginia.

THE MALL.
An aerial perspective of the Mall as seen from the Potomac River. The expansive Mall is defined on the Potomac side by the three presidential memorials to George Washington, Abraham Lincoln, and Thomas Jefferson.

Captain John Smith of the Jamestown Colony first explored the Potomac River in 1608, recording in his travel chronicle an image of pristine beauty and extraordinary bounty. The fish, he told his compatriots in England, were "lying so thicke with their heads above water" that "we attempted to catch them with a frying pan." These same bountiful supplies of fish, crabs, and oysters had supplied countless generations of Native Americans in the Potomac watershed. These original inhabitants had long ago established villages along the river, engaged in agriculture, trapped for beaver pelts, and mined nearby quartzite quarries for tools and weapons. European settlers, following in the wake of Captain Smith's discovery, soon found the Potomac region to be rich in potential for farming, the pursuit of commercial trade, and the forging of new cities—including the eventual site for the District of Columbia, the capital of the United States of America.

The word *Potomac* first appeared on Captain Smith's 1608 map as "Patawomeck," perhaps an obscure reference to the Pawtomax Indians, who once lived near the confluence of the Shenandoah and Potomac rivers. Captain Smith—and the

Jamestown colonists who visited the "Patawomack" at the dawn of the seventeenth century—were seeking gold and a possible outlet to the "South Seas." Their ignorance of the geography of the Potomac River and its tributaries was profound, but the journey nonetheless became a harbinger for future settlement in the region.

Often called the "Nation's River," the Potomac occupies a special place in the American national consciousness. Mount Vernon, the majestic home of George Washington, still overlooks the historic waterway on the southern approach to the District of Columbia. Other magnificent monuments hug the banks of the Potomac—the Lincoln Memorial, the Washington Monument, the Jefferson Memorial, and Arlington National Cemetery. The river flows through blood-drenched territory where Union and Confederate armies once marched and fought in the American Civil War. Cities, towns, forests, and scenic parks mingle today along the undulating 380-mile course of the Potomac River as it makes its relentless passage from a small spring in West Virginia to the Chesapeake Bay.

The Potomac River drains an area of over 14,600 square miles. The northern branch forms a natural boundary between West Virginia and Maryland from

(TOP)
THE JOHN F. KENNEDY CENTER.
The John F. Kennedy Center for the Performing Arts, designed by Edward Durell Stone. A "living memorial" to the assassinated president, the Kennedy Center is an important cultural landmark in the nation's capital, housing the Eisenhower Theater, the Concert Hall, and the Opera House.

(LEFT)
ROWING ON THE POTOMAC.
Rowers with their sculls are a familiar presence on the Potomac River, as seen here at sunrise. The Washington Canoe Club is housed on the Potomac River near Key Bridge.

(RIGHT)
THE TERRACE FOUNTAINS.
The illuminated Terrace Fountains of the Kennedy Center for the Performing Arts.

(ABOVE)
BUST OF JOHN F. KENNEDY AT THE KENNEDY CENTER.
Robert Berks' bust of John F. Kennedy, a portrait in bronze of the namesake of Washington's premier theater and concert hall.

(RIGHT)
ARLINGTON MEMORIAL BRIDGE SCULPTURE.
Equestrian sculptures symbolizing the Arts of Peace and sculpted by James Earle Fraser adorn the entrance to the Arlington Memorial Bridge. The bridge is one of Washington's most beautiful, offering a majestic link across the Potomac from the Lincoln Memorial to Arlington National Cemetery on the Virginia side.

(LEFT)
THE ARLINGTON MEMORIAL BRIDGE.
The majestic Lincoln Memorial dominates the approach to the Arlington Memorial Bridge, linking the District of Columbia with Virginia.

The Memorial Bridge consists of nine low arches, reminiscent of a Roman aqueduct.

(OPPOSITE)
THE WATERGATE COMPLEX.
The Watergate apartment and restaurant complex in Washington, named for the band shell and restaurant that once occupied the spot on the shore of the Potomac River.

The Watergate is remembered for the 1972 break-in that led to the resignation of President Richard Nixon.

the river's source at Fairfax Stone to Harpers Ferry, West Virginia. The southward direction of the Potomac beyond Harpers Ferry, the historic site of John Brown's raid, defines the boundary between Virginia and Maryland. As the Potomac snakes its way to the sea, several major tributaries join it: the Shenandoah at Harpers Ferry; the Monocacy in the Piedmont area; the Anacostia at Washington, D.C.; and the St. Mary's in southern Maryland. Once the Potomac cascades through a series of rapids and falls, the most dramatic located at Great Falls with a cataract of 35 feet, it abruptly becomes highly navigable, enlarging to 11 miles wide at Point Lookout, Maryland, where it empties into the Chesapeake Bay.

Crossing the ornate Memorial Bridge connecting the Lincoln Memorial to Arlington National Cemetery on the Virginia side, one senses the primary role of the Potomac River in defining the character and mood of the city. Essential reference points for Washington—geographic, historical, and cultural—are inextricably linked to the river. A monumental city has been and will continue to be shaped by its riverscape.

Georgetown, once a small village on the Potomac, is now a celebrated and upscale precinct of Washington, D.C. Settled nearly a half century before the Federal City was established, Georgetown became a prosperous trading center, boasting an impressive ensemble of shops, inns, and churches. At the terminus of the Chesapeake and Ohio Canal, Georgetown was on the banks of the headwaters of the Potomac, a convenient inland port for the tobacco trade in the formative years of the United States. Today Georgetown claims special status for its upscale historic homes, Georgetown University, and numerous cultural institutions. No precinct in the nation's capital can rival the excitement and flair of modern-day Georgetown.

Two landmarks on the Potomac River near Georgetown stand out: the Kennedy Center for the Performing Arts and the Watergate complex. Built in 1971, the Kennedy Center has drawn praise and criticism for its architecture, but few have denied its cultural impact on the city. Its proximity to the river, willow-shaded terrace, spacious entrance plaza, and profusion of marble, bronze, and crystal appointments impart a unique ambience to the Kennedy Center.

Nearby is the legendary Watergate with its offices and apartments, the scene of the botched burglary in 1972 that led ultimately to a scandal that compelled Richard Nixon to resign the American presidency.

(LEFT)

ARLINGTON HOUSE AND THE GRAVE OF JOHN F. KENNEDY. *Arlington House, once the home of Robert E. Lee, overlooks the simple grave of President John F. Kennedy (1917–1963) at Arlington National Cemetery.*

Nearby is the grave of Robert F. Kennedy (1925–1968), which is marked only by a simple white cross.

The name "Watergate" itself may be traced to the ill-fated project in the 1930s to construct a symbolic water gate to the city near the Lincoln Memorial. The project never materialized, but during World War II a large barge was moored there and served as a convenient spot for summer concerts for decades—at a time before the Kennedy Center was constructed.

From the Virginia side, Robert E. Lee's Arlington mansion, situated on a hilltop, offers a panoramic view of the Mall. The Washington Monument, Smithsonian museums, Lincoln Memorial, and Capitol Hill define this core precinct. No skyscrapers punctuate the cityscape, but the sense of a planned city is evident. The layout of streets and circles, the grandiose government buildings, public parks, and museums mirror the extraordinary majesty and beauty of the nation's capital. The neo-classical Memorial Bridge with its balustrades, equestrian statues, roadway, and sidewalks provides a vital and symbolic link across the Potomac River.

Arlington National Cemetery is a sacred spot situated on 420 acres where some 200,000 war dead are buried. The tree-dominated cemetery includes the Tomb of the Unknowns, which bears the familiar inscription, "Here rests in honored glory an American soldier known but to God." Nearby flat stones mark the graves of unknowns added later from World War II and the Korean and Vietnam wars.

President John F. Kennedy's grave is located on a beautiful hillside beneath a slab of fieldstone brought from Cape Cod in his native Massachusetts. The Kennedy grave conveys a mood of stark simplicity consistent with the larger architecture of Arlington National Cemetery: only an eternal flame adorns the burial site. President Kennedy's wife Jacqueline Kennedy is buried on this same plot. Nearby is the separate grave of his slain brother, Robert F. Kennedy. From this elevated point, the Washington Monument may be seen in the distance across the Potomac River.

Looking across the Potomac from Arlington National Cemetery, visitors see other war memorials. Most notable of these memorials— and a powerful attraction for all who live in or visit Washington—is the striking Vietnam Veterans Memorial, fashioned in black granite in close proximity to the Lincoln Memorial. The Korean War and, most recently, World War II also have been honored with monuments on the Mall.

The Virginia side of the Potomac is home to the Pentagon, the legendary headquarters of the

Department of Defense. Located on what was once an airport, the Pentagon is a multi-level, ringed administrative building with more than 3.7 million square feet of office space. The federal government built the Pentagon during the national emergency of World War II, at a time when military affairs assumed an enlarged role in American life. The Pentagon is a city unto itself, employing more than 23,000 people, military and civilian. As a symbol of American military power, the Pentagon was targeted for destruction by terrorists on September 11, 2001. The stunning attack resulted in a tragic loss of life and massive material damage to one wing of the Pentagon, but the structure was quickly repaired and once again assumed its customary role as the center for the American military in the twenty-first century.

Old Town Alexandria, Virginia, is situated on the Potomac River near the Woodrow Wilson Bridge. Founded in 1732 by Scottish merchants, the port town eventually became an important terminus for the tobacco trade, even being considered at one point as a candidate for the new capital of the United States. The historical importance of Alexandria is tied to George Washington, who maintained a separate home in Alexandria, just a few miles upriver from his estate at Mount Vernon.

Today Alexandria is an affluent suburban community with a unique identity. As a city, Alexandria is keenly aware of its own heritage, which predates Washington, D.C., located just eight miles away. Alexandria is a river town, with its distinctive downtown area known as Old Town still conveying the look of colonial America: brick sidewalks, cobblestone streets, and old Christ Church, where George Washington once worshipped. Other landmarks such as the Carlyle House and Gadsby's Tavern possess links with colonial American history. Like Georgetown, Alexandria boasts numerous shops, retail establishments, restaurants, and pubs. On the east boundary of Old Town is a busy two-mile Potomac waterfront, anchored by the famed Torpedo Factory Art Gallery.

In fair weather, cruise boats depart from Alexandria's waterfront for leisurely passage up and down the Potomac River, offering breathtaking views of the nation's capital and such historic sites as Mount Vernon.

Seeing the city of Washington, D.C., from the perspective of the Potomac River, David Tuvill's proverb comes to mind: "Nature made the fields and man the cities."

(LEFT)

THE PENTAGON.
The Pentagon, situated on the Virginia side of the Potomac River, is the symbol of American military power. Under one roof, reputed to be the largest office complex in the world, the Pentagon oversees the vast American military establishment based at home and abroad.

(TOP)

"THE PRESIDENT'S OWN."
A member of the United States Marine Corps Band, in full dress uniform with white gloves, proudly wears the insignia "The President's Own." The Marine band, as well as other bands in the armed forces, performs frequently at public ceremonies in Washington, D.C.

(OPPOSITE)

THE U.S. MARINE CORPS WAR MEMORIAL.
A dramatic view of the U.S. Marine Corps War Memorial (popularly known as the Iwo Jima Memorial), sculpted by Felix W. de Weldon. The large statue brings to life the celebrated photograph by newsman Joe Rosenthal of Marines raising the American flag atop Mount Suribachi on Iwo Jima in 1945.

(OPPOSITE AND LEFT)

THE JEFFERSON MEMORIAL AND THE TIDAL BASIN.
Cherry blossoms herald the arrival of spring at the Tidal Basin. President Franklin D. Roosevelt led the campaign in the 1930s to build the tribute in white marble to Thomas Jefferson. The classical domed structure was designed by architect John Russell Pope and modeled on the Roman Pantheon. The first cherry trees planted around the Tidal Basin were a gift of the Japanese government.

(ABOVE)

THE JEFFERSON MEMORIAL STATUE.
Thomas Jefferson's towering image, sculpted by Rudolph Evans, is the centerpiece in the Jefferson Memorial, dedicated in 1943 on the occasion of the two-hundredth birthday of the third president of the United States.

(OPPOSITE)

**THE ALEXANDRIA
WATERFRONT.**
*The city of Alexandria was a
tobacco port on the Potomac
River in colonial times.
Today, Alexandria is part of
Metropolitan Washington, and
is a lively business, shopping,
and residential community
with its own distinct history
and personality.*

(THIS PAGE)

**ARCHITECTURE IN
ALEXANDRIA.**
*Alexandria is filled with
historic churches, most
notably Christ Church
Episcopal (LEFT), the home
parish of George Washington.
Eighteenth-century townhouses
(Captain's Row) grace
Princess Street (RIGHT),
a surviving cobblestone street
from colonial Alexandria.*

(LEFT)

GADSBY'S TAVERN, ALEXANDRIA.
Gadsby's Tavern in Alexandria was named after Englishman John Gadsby, who operated the historic tavern from 1796 to 1808. Gadsby's celebrated patrons included George Washington, John Adams, Thomas Jefferson, James Madison, and the Marquis de Lafayette.

(RIGHT)

THE OLD APOTHECARY SHOP, ALEXANDRIA.
The Old Apothecary Shop represents a link to life in colonial America.

(OPPOSITE)

"THE OLD GUARD."
Members of the U.S. Army Third Infantry Regiment, "The Old Guard," here reenact a drill at Mount Vernon.

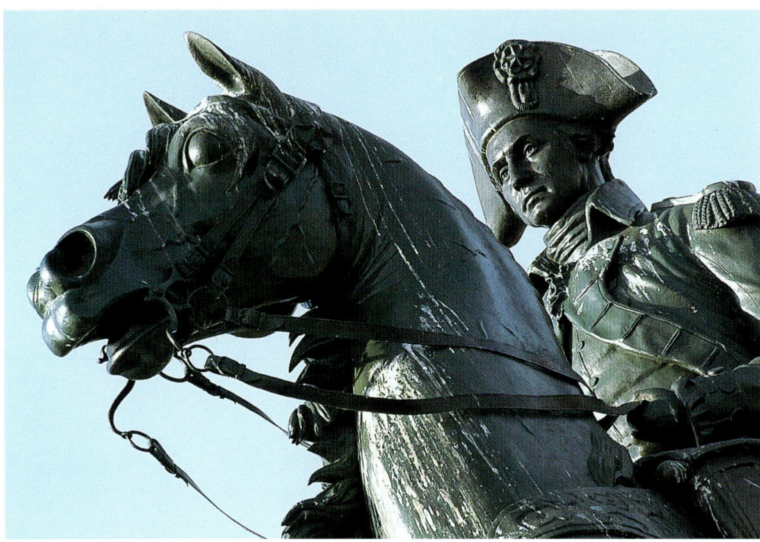

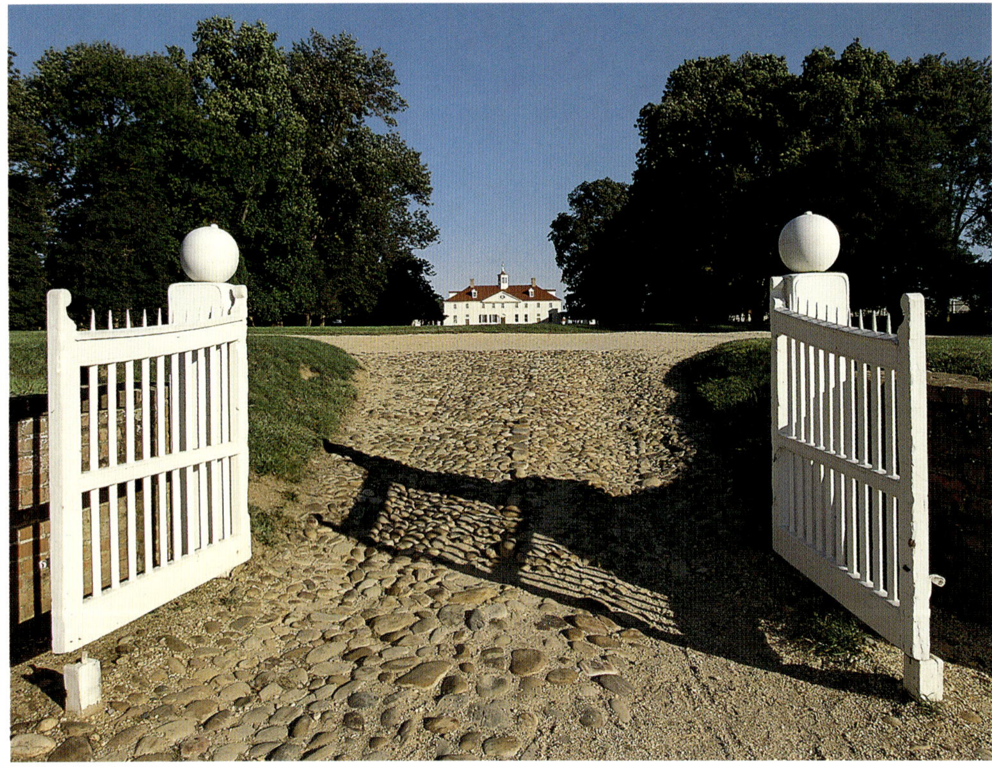

(TOP)
STATUE OF GEORGE WASHINGTON.
An equestrian statue of George Washington, hero of the American Revolution and first president of the United States, at Mount Vernon.

(BOTTOM)
GATE AT MOUNT VERNON.
White picket gates frame George Washington's Mount Vernon mansion on the Potomac River.

(RIGHT)
MOUNT VERNON ESTATE.
Mount Vernon, the beloved home of George Washington, occupies an elevated spot overlooking the Potomac River. The lovely Mount Vernon mansion once stood at the center of an estate numbering more than 8,000 acres, a vast plantation divided into five separate farms. Mount Vernon also houses the grave of George Washington.

(OPPOSITE)
GEORGE WASHINGTON'S STUDY.
George Washington's spacious, sunlit office at his Mount Vernon home.

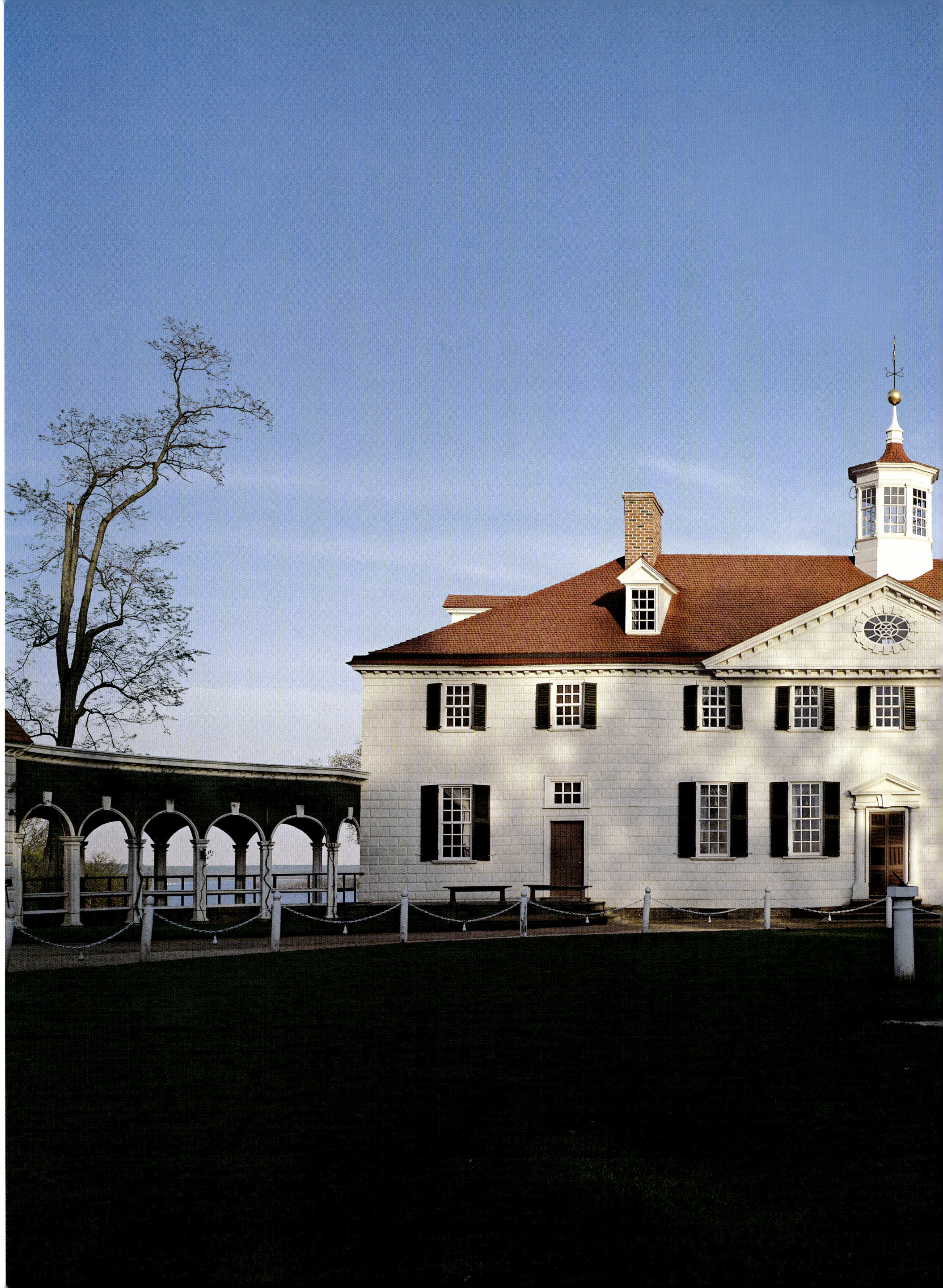

(LEFT)

FORMAL DINING ROOM AT MOUNT VERNON.
The elegant formal dining room, or "new room," at George Washington's Mount Vernon plantation overlooking the Potomac River.

(ABOVE)

MOUNT VERNON GARDENS.
Today the Mount Vernon estate preserves 30 acres of walled ornamental gardens, lawns, and wooded plots, including some poplar trees and boxwood hedges planted by George Washington in the eighteenth century.

(OPPOSITE)

AERIAL VIEW OF MOUNT VERNON.
Mount Vernon, George Washington's beloved refuge from war and the rigors of public service, is nestled in a forested plot overlooking the Potomac River.

GEORGETOWN

– FROM THE POEM "GEORGETOWN GHOSTS"
BY WILLIAM TIPTON TABLOTT

TWO HOUR
PARKING
7 AM-6:30 PM
2 PERMIT
HOLDERS EXCEPTED

(ABOVE AND RIGHT)
THE C & O CANAL.
*A canal barge preserves
Georgetown's past glory as a
terminus to the Chesapeake
and Ohio Canal. Today the old
towpaths along the canal are
magnets for joggers, bicyclists,
and fishermen. To reenact the
canal era, a passenger pulls
on a rope to move her
slow-moving barge down
the canal. The C & O Canal
prospered in the early decades
of the nineteenth century until
it was eclipsed by the railroads.*

(FOLDOUT)
GEORGETOWN UNIVERSITY.
*Founded in 1789, Georgetown
University's spires tower above
the Potomac River.*

(PANORAMA)
ROW HOUSES.
*Row houses grace a street in
Georgetown, a community
known for its architectural
tradition and unique
personality.*

Older than Washington, D.C., Georgetown prospered as a small port town in Maryland in colonial America, linked to the flourishing tobacco trade. In the aftermath of the American Revolution, the Founding Fathers gave some initial consideration to Georgetown as the site for the new national capital. However, they ultimately selected the expansive rolling hill country adjacent to Georgetown as the home for the new Federal City.

Those who visited rustic Georgetown in the colonial era have left divergent, often conflicting, images of life in the small town on the Potomac. Abigail Adams, the wife of President John Adams, described Georgetown in colorful terms as little more than a "dirty little hole." James Kent, writing in 1793, caught the essential charm of the "pleasant village situated on waving hills on the North side of the Potomack," noting the "noble view" Georgetown offered of the river and the many attractive hillside houses "exceedingly well built of brick." Much of the genteel atmosphere Kent first observed in eighteenth-century America persists today in modern-day Georgetown.

Early visitors discerned another key dimension of social life in Georgetown, the studied sense of separateness (for some, aloofness). First laid out as a community in 1751 and then incorporated in 1789, the residents of Georgetown cultivated a peculiar identity of their own, even with the advent and growth of the Federal City nearby. Most of the citizenry of Georgetown took great pride in Georgetown's economic prosperity as a port city exporting tobacco and importing luxury goods from Europe. In those days, only a dirt gravel road (later known as Pennsylvania Avenue) connected Georgetown with the president's mansion and the Federal City.

During the nineteenth century, however, Georgetown fell on hard times, losing much of its mercantile prosperity and finding itself overwhelmed by Washington, D.C. The old Chesapeake and Ohio Canal, which had been the source of great wealth, fell into a period of decline with railroads becoming the dominant form of commercial transport. The Potomac silted up, choking off what remained of the once vital trade on the river. In time, Georgetown even lost its autonomy, being annexed by the more flourishing and ever-expanding Federal City. Even for a time, Georgetown became known as "West Washington." The long spiral into urban decline persisted into the 1930s, but with the advent of Franklin Roosevelt's New Deal, the pattern was slowly reversed. Today, Georgetown reflects a new vitality and prosperity, having recaptured its special identity within the boundaries of Washington, D.C.

One charming remnant of Georgetown's past glory is the towpath on the old Chesapeake and Ohio Canal, a 22-mile man-made waterway no longer filled with canal boats, but a powerful magnet for hikers and cyclists. The old C & O Canal towpath also connects cyclists with other towpaths for excursions beyond the District of Columbia. Seeing the old canal locks and lockkeepers' houses prompts in all visitors an appreciation for Georgetown's pre-modern life as a major trading center on the Potomac.

The towering Healy Building on the campus of Georgetown University dominates the skyline of Georgetown. The 200-foot clock tower offers a signature image for the famed Jesuit school. Other buildings on the Georgetown campus continue to attract public notice as architectural gems, in particular the Joseph Mark Lauinger Memorial Library and the Old North Building. Few universities can match the elevated beauty of Georgetown University.

Another institution situated atop a hill in Georgetown is the famed Dumbarton Oaks estate, now the home for Harvard University's Dumbarton Oaks Research Library and Collections (with special research programs and art collections related to Byzantine and pre-Columbian history). A museum, designed by Philip Johnson, houses Dumbarton Oak's world-renowned pre-Columbian art collection, an extraordinary collection once owned by Robert and Mildred Bliss. A 10-acre terraced garden of stunning beauty, laid out by Mildred Bliss between 1921 and 1941, draws countless visitors to Dumbarton Oaks each year. The original house has undergone numerous renovations and expansions since 1829. The highly ornate Music Room at Dumbarton Oaks has been the locale for memorial performances by such renowned artists as Wanda Landowska, Lucrezia Bori, Igor Stravinsky, and Ignace Paderewski.

Called "America's most civilized square mile" by planner Carl Feiss, Dumbarton Oaks has played a pivotal role in shaping war and peace in the twentieth century. Few visitors today are fully aware of the fact that the reading room at Dumbarton Oaks, once a bedroom, served as the

(ABOVE)
THE OLD STONE HOUSE.
The interior of the Old Stone House, Georgetown's oldest surviving structure, built by Christopher Leyman around 1765. The National Park Service maintains the building as a museum, offering a portrait of life in pre-Revolutionary America.

(LEFT)
BUFFALO BRIDGE.
A detail from the Dumbarton Bridge at Q Street, adorned with sculptor A. P. Proctor's sandstone heads modeled on Kicking Bear, chief of the Sioux nation. The bridge with its battlements crosses Rock Creek Park, one of the most extensive public parks in Washington, D.C.

A GEORGETOWN WINTER.
*Snow-covered Wisconsin
Avenue attracts walkers in
Georgetown after a severe
winter storm in 1979.
Washington often experiences
the extremes of weather—hot,
humid summers and occasional
blizzards in winter.*

(RIGHT)

THE 1789 RESTAURANT.
*Interior of the "1789
Restaurant" in Georgetown.
Part of a complex of three
restaurants, the 1789
Restaurant evokes the
ambience of an elegant home,
appointed with antiques, fine
china service, and period
furnishings.*

(OPPOSITE)

**AERIAL VIEW
OF GEORGETOWN.**
*An aerial view of Georgetown
shows the residential character
of the community. Georgetown
boasts an abundance of trees,
and some of the most beautiful
homes, row houses, and
apartment complexes in
Washington. Georgetown
was a prosperous port town
in the eighteenth century prior
to the establishment of the
Federal City.*

initial meeting place for the Manhattan Project,
the plan to build the atom bomb in World War II.
During that same war Dumbarton Oaks hosted a
pivotal diplomatic conference in 1944 that led to
the establishment of the United Nations.

Other sites in Georgetown offer concrete
links to the past. Situated in the midst of
residential Georgetown is the "1789 Restaurant."
The building complex contains three separate
restaurants—the 1789 Restaurant, The Tombs, and
F. Scott's. Just one of many excellent restaurants
in Georgetown, the 1789 Restaurant evokes
several historical themes in its name—the
memorable year in which the Constitution of the
United States was adopted, George Washington
assumed the presidency, and Archbishop John
Carroll purchased the elevated plot of land on
which he built Georgetown University.

The face of Georgetown has been transformed
over the centuries, but certain older homes
survive as vivid reminders of an earlier time. The
"Old Stone House," located on M Street (once
called Bridge Street), is one sterling example of
historic preservation. Built around 1765, the
stone house claims the honor of being the oldest
standing building in Washington, D.C.

Christopher Laymen, the original owner, built his
home with a lavish use of blue granite extracted
from a local quarry. Purchased by the United
States in 1953, the Old Stone House is an
excellent example of pre-Revolutionary
vernacular architecture.

The old Flour Mill, built in 1845, offers the
visitor a sense of Georgetown in the heyday of
the C & O Canal. The Mill building is the sole
survivor of a cluster of mills and warehouses that
once were a part of Georgetown's mercantile
district. Reflecting a different time, the old Flour
Mill, now expanded and renovated, is a modern-
day condominium complex.

A more dramatic representation of modern
Georgetown is the Washington Harbor complex,
built in 1986. The advent of the huge waterfront
cluster of shops, condominiums, and offices
became one of the most important architectural
developments in the 1980s. Designed by Arthur
Cotton Moore, Washington Harbor incorporates
many architectural themes with its domes,
columns, asymmetrical levels, and myriad façades.
The building of Washington Harbor signaled a
modern architectural renaissance in Georgetown.
Nearby are other shopping centers to attract locals

and visitors—the Georgetown Market (a town public market since 1795) and Georgetown Park (an upscale shopping complex located on the site that was once the hub for Georgetown's streetcars).

One of the most distinctive bridges connecting Georgetown to Washington, D.C., proper is the Dumbarton or the so-called Buffalo Bridge. The elaborate bridge can be viewed from Rock Creek Valley, and evokes a powerful image with its massive arches, battlements, and stone adornments. At the ends of the bridge stand four buffalos, sculpted by Alexander Phimister Proctor in 1914, the same man who also contributed four tigers to adorn the 16th Street Bridge. The Buffalo Bridge is the connecting link, over Rock Creek Park, from Georgetown to the Embassy Row section of Dupont Circle. Sometimes the bridge is called the "Q Street" bridge to suggest its link to Embassy Row.

Another major bridge in Georgetown is the Key Bridge, linking the District of Columbia to Rosslyn on the Virginia side. Named after the composer of the National Anthem, Francis Scott Key, the bridge today is a major thoroughfare for commuter traffic. Few people realize that Francis Scott Key was a longtime resident of Georgetown,

a lawyer, and three times U.S. Attorney for the District of Columbia. Below the present-day Key Bridge, one can see the remnants of the old Aqueduct Bridge, once a cast-iron bridge that provided a rail and carriage passageway across the Potomac (and an aqueduct supplying water to the District). Rump stone arches still rise above the surface of the Potomac where the Aqueduct Bridge once stood in the nineteenth century.

"I believe there are scarcely any places in the world, more beautiful, and better situated," Christophe DeGraffenried observed, when he visited the Potomac River near Georgetown in 1712. His remarks still ring true after the passing of centuries and Georgetown's own transformation into a vital precinct of Washington, D.C.

(ABOVE AND LEFT)
GEORGETOWN HOMES.
Inside the elegant homes of newspaper editor Ben Bradlee (ABOVE) and architect Warren Cox (LEFT).

(OPPOSITE)
WINTER IN GEORGETOWN.
Streetlights illuminate a Georgetown home in the depth of winter. The streets in Georgetown are narrow and tree-shaded, always a striking scene during a snowstorm.

(ABOVE)

DUMBARTON OAKS.
Robert and Mildred Bliss purchased Dumbarton Oaks in 1920. Today the estate houses Harvard University's research center and museum devoted to Byzantine history, pre-Columbian art and culture, and landscape architecture.

The terraced gardens at Dumbarton Oaks, together with a larger complex of "garden rooms" and woods, represent a gem in American landscape architecture.

(RIGHT)

PRE-COLUMBIAN ART EXHIBIT.
Artifacts at the pre-Columbian collection at Dumbarton Oaks, exhibited in the museum annex designed by Philip Johnson and opened in the 1960s.

(OPPOSITE TOP)

FOUNTAIN TERRACE.
Surrounded by blossoming chrysanthemums, a putti with a dolphin in the Fountain Terrace at Dumbarton Oaks.

(OPPOSITE BOTTOM)

PEBBLE GARDEN.
A shallow pool in the Pebble Garden at Dumbarton Oaks, with elaborate patterns created from multicolored pebbles.

(LEFT)

GEORGETOWN SHOPS.
Georgetown is widely known for its mercantile district and shopping areas. Pictured here is Georgetown Park, a re-creation of a Victorian shopping arcade.

(ABOVE)

GEORGETOWN UNIVERSITY TOWER.
The distinctive Healy Building at Georgetown University, named after Father Patrick Healy, the first African-American to earn a doctorate and become president of Georgetown University. The 200-foot Healy tower is one of Georgetown's signature structures.

(RIGHT)

WASHINGTON HARBOR.
Built in the 1980s, Washington Harbor represented a major effort to revitalize the Georgetown waterfront. An unusual mix of façades and levels, the large-scale complex is the home of offices, shops, and condominiums.

DOWNTOWN

"The city is not a concrete jungle,
it is a human zoo."
— DESMOND MORRIS

WASHINGTON'S CONVENTION CENTER.
Washington's Convention Center, completed in 2003, has made the nation's capital an attractive meeting place for conventions, trade shows, and concerts. The center is the largest building in Washington, D.C., covering six city blocks, the equivalent of six football fields.

THE UNDERGROUND METRO SYSTEM.
A modern and highly efficient subway system links the Downtown section with outlying cities and communities in the Metropolitan Washington area.

DOWNTOWN MURAL.
Art plays a vital role in expressing the character and personality of Washington, as shown here in Stiletto, painted by G. Byron Peck on the side of Asia Nora's Restaurant on M Street in Downtown.

DOWNTOWN WASHINGTON.
An aerial view of downtown Washington at the convergence of Florida and Connecticut avenues. Washington has maintained the long tradition of prohibiting skyscrapers and high-rise buildings.

Well into the twentieth century, most inhabitants of Washington, D.C., lived within the confines of Pierre L'Enfant's original Federal City, inside what became known as the "downtown" section, framed by the Potomac and Anacostia rivers. For generations, the urban core of "Washington City" was not coextensive with the District of Columbia, with larger portions of the territory of the District given over to residential and farm use. The 1930s and 1940s, however, signaled a dramatic transformation—a quickened pace of growth and urban sprawl that dramatically altered the contours and character of the nation's capital. Telescoped into this extraordinary era were two powerful agents of social change: Franklin Roosevelt's New Deal and World War II. Modern Washington, D.C., as we now know it in the twenty-first century, may be traced to this historical watershed in the American experience.

As the population of Washington mushroomed, mass flight to the suburbs, especially in the decades following World War II, became the dominant pattern. The advent of "Greater Washington" meant increasing urban sprawl, where government workers often lived in distant locales well beyond the Beltway and deep in formerly rural areas of Maryland and Virginia. While in times past you could capture a photo of Washington from a balloon or an airplane, today satellite imagery is required to comprehend visually the geographical footprint of Metropolitan Washington.

Washington grew horizontally, for certain, but urban planning for the nation's capital still followed the logic of L'Enfant's original blueprint. One key and enduring governing principle for urban planning has been the embrace of strict limits on building heights, a prohibition on skyscrapers that arose at the turn of the twentieth century and endures to this day. The near-Earth skyline of Washington stood in sharp contrast to those of New York City or Chicago. The downtown section of the capital increasingly was given over to government structures, offices, hotels, theaters, and shops—all at the expense of private residences. As Washington grew, the downtown precinct reflected this urban trend in a powerful way.

Defining the boundaries of Downtown defies precision, especially in more recent decades as the footprint of government buildings, shops, restaurants, and other commercial enterprises

(FAR LEFT AND OPPOSITE)
DOWNTOWN MURALS:
A celebration of the arts: a mural of a cresting ocean wave (LEFT), combines the classic beauty of downtown with the modern flair of the twenty-first century (FAR LEFT). John Bailey's mural of Marilyn Monroe is a striking creation on the side of a downtown building.

(ABOVE)
THE CHINATOWN GATE.
When Beijing, China, and Washington became "sister cities" in 1986, China donated the colorful Chinese gate at 7th and H streets. The colorful arch reflects the architecture of pre-modern China's Qing Dynasty (1649–1911).

THE U.S. NAVY MEMORIAL.
The plaza in front of the U.S. Navy Memorial on Pennsylvania Avenue contains a projection of Earth fashioned in granite. Established in 1977, the memorial honors all who have served at sea. The memorial finds its inspiration in Pierre L'Enfant's original design for the nation's capital.

PENNSYLVANIA AVENUE.
Looking eastward from 15th Street, the Capitol is visible at the far end of Pennsylvania Avenue. One of Washington's famous streets, Pennsylvania Avenue links Capitol Hill and the White House and is lined with such historic buildings as the National Archives, the Old Post Office, and the Willard Hotel.

expanded dramatically. For much of Washington's history, the stretch of land from the Treasury Building to 7th Street arguably was the downtown section of the city. One of the reasons why this particular area attracted businesses was its elevation, a strip of territory well above the marshy lowland of the Mall. Modern-day visitors to the Mall do not realize how inhospitable this section was to horse and carriage traffic in pre-modern times. As a result, Pennsylvania Avenue, for example, became the preferred locale for banks, shops, and office buildings. With the advent of the twenty-first century, the downtown has seen the growth of new apartment and condominium complexes, signaling a return of residential housing to the historic core of the city.

The venerable Willard Hotel still stands in this special precinct of Washington, for decades a favorite residence for congressmen, newspapermen, and writers. The Willard is linked with more than one important person in the history of the United States. In the dark hours of the Civil War, Julia Ward Howe composed the "Battle Hymn of the Republic" in her room at the hotel. It would also be in one room of the Willard that Martin Luther King, Jr., wrote his memorable "I Have a Dream" speech. The present building reflects the redesign work undertaken in 1901. At one point the old hotel was closed, and then threatened with the wrecking ball. The venerable old structure was saved by the intervention of the Pennsylvania Avenue Development Corporation. The old Willard reopened in 1986 as one of Washington's most fashionable hotels.

Farther down Pennsylvania Avenue and hugging the Mall area near the National Gallery of Art is another survivor from an earlier time, the Sears House (in reality three structures, including the Apex, Brady, and Gilman buildings). The Sears House is a whimsical design with its twin towers and flamboyant lines. Mathew Brady, the famed photographer of the Civil War, once had his main studio in the rear of the building.

Today many other architectural gems survive in the downtown area. One of the great masterpieces of the nineteenth century, a most eccentric structure that now houses the National Building Museum, is the old Pension Building. Located at 4th and F streets, the Pension Building was completed in 1885, prompting immediate derision for its unusual silhouette

and red brick façade. The building's designer, General Montgomery Meigs, took his inspiration from Michelangelo's Palazzo Farnese in Rome. The original purpose of the building was to provide space for the administration of pensions for Civil War veterans. The frieze, running along all sides of the Pension Building, depicts various heroic episodes in the history of the Union Army. The awe-inspiring inner chamber of the Pension Building contains four ringed arcades supported by mammoth 75-foot Corinthian columns. Scorned by contemporary critics, the building was dismissed as "Meigs' Old Red Barn." Civil War General William Tecumseh Sherman adopted a rather harsh posture toward the architectural wonder, remarking, "The worst of it is, it is fireproof." Once a candidate for demolition, the Pension Building today is considered a national landmark and is always a coveted venue for a presidential inaugural ball.

Ford's Theater on 10th Street occupies a special and tragic place in the history of the nation's capital. It was here on April 14, 1865, that John Wilkes Booth assassinated President Abraham Lincoln. Booth was a popular actor in his day and a fervent supporter of the Confederate cause in the Civil War, believing that the murder of President Lincoln would throw the country into political crisis and save the South from defeat. Booth himself was shot while attempting to escape and those involved in the conspiracy were later executed or imprisoned. John T. Ford, an entrepreneur from Baltimore, built the popular theater in 1861, the year the Civil War began. With the assassination of Lincoln, Ford's theatrical house fell on hard times, and in 1866, he sold the structure to the federal government. Today the National Park Service oversees the restored theater, which offers visitors a dramatic opportunity to see an important place in Civil War Washington.

Other Civil War-era buildings in the downtown area have been adapted over time for use as museums. One extraordinary example is the Renwick Gallery, located near the White House on 17th Street and Pennsylvania Avenue. James Renwick, the famed architect, originally designed the building to house the art collection belonging to William Wilson Corcoran. The collection was later moved to another, larger museum building, the present Corcoran Gallery of Art on 17th Street. Today the Renwick

continues as an art museum of the Smithsonian Institution.

Downtown Washington took on an international flavor in 1986 with the construction of the Chinatown Gateway, a gift of the People's Republic of China. A mammoth arch 47 feet high and 61 feet wide, the so-called Friendship Gate is a testament to the special relationship between sister cities Beijing and Washington. The highly ornate gate, mirroring the architecture of the Qing Dynasty, is built with modern materials and situated in a bustling area of Washington.

Another striking building, the National Geographic Society headquarters, follows many modern themes in twentieth-century American architecture. Located at 17th Street and M Street, at the very center of Washington, the headquarters building is a blend of old and new, the 1987 renovation of a 1902 structure.

Dupont Circle, the intersection of Massachusetts, Connecticut, and New Hampshire avenues, lies just outside, but in close proximity to, the historic downtown section. In fact, this vibrant and cosmopolitan neighborhood is considered by some as functionally downtown in terms of its role in the life of the nation's capital.

Once considered the "Fashionable West End," Dupont Circle was the home of palatial mansions built by wealthy tycoons at the end of the nineteenth century. The side streets linked to Dupont Circle became the home to middle-class citizens, who often lived in three- and four-story row houses. Today Dupont Circle proper, with its distinctive fountain by sculptor Daniel Chester French, is a magnet for office workers, mothers with strollers, musicians, chess players, bicycle messengers, and locals walking to the nearby Metrorail stop.

The vibrant and expansive Downtown is the heart of the political, social, and commercial life of the nation's capital.

(OPPOSITE)

FORD'S THEATER.

An exterior view of Ford's Theater, where John Wilkes Booth assassinated President Abraham Lincoln. Today the theater is maintained by the National Park Service.

(LEFT)

ABRAHAM LINCOLN'S THEATER BOX.

The box where Lincoln was seated the night he was shot by John Wilkes Booth.

(ABOVE)

JOHN WILKES BOOTH'S PISTOL.

The Derringer .44-caliber pistol used by John Wilkes Booth to kill Lincoln with a single shot.

(RIGHT)

PETERSEN HOUSE.

After Lincoln was shot, he was taken to the Petersen House, directly across 10th Street from Ford's Theater. He died there on the night of April 14, 1865.

(OPPOSITE)
THE PENN SEARS BUILDING.
The twin-towered Sears Building on Pennsylvania Avenue is a three-building complex (Apex, Brady, and Gilman structures). Mathew Brady, famed Civil War photographer, once had his office and studio in this building complex. Abraham Lincoln came to the Brady studios for his last portrait photograph.

(LEFT)
THE WILLARD HOTEL.
The grand lobby of the twelve-story Willard Hotel on Pennsylvania Avenue, arguably Washington's finest hostelry.

(ABOVE)
THE RENWICK GALLERY.
Designed by architect James Renwick, the building known today as the Renwick Gallery was originally constructed in 1859 to house the art collection of financier William Wilson Corcoran. The venerable Renwick Gallery is part of the Smithsonian Institution and is dedicated to American decorative arts.

FREDERICK DOUGLASS.
A portrait of Frederick Douglass at the Frederick Douglass Historic site. A former slave, Douglass became a powerful abolitionist leader and spokesman for racial equality during the eras of the Civil War and Reconstruction.

(LEFT)
THE FREDERICK DOUGLASS HOUSE.
The Frederick Douglass House, also called Cedar Hill, is located on W Street in southeast Washington. The historic home is maintained by the National Park Service. Douglass moved to the nation's capital from Rochester, New York, in 1872, first to the Capitol Hill area and then to Cedar Hill in 1878.

(RIGHT)
INSIDE THE FREDERICK DOUGLASS HOUSE.
The Cedar Hill home of Frederick Douglass is filled with period furniture and antiques, including his personal belongings, library, and a portrait of Joseph Cinque, who led a rebellion on the slave ship Amistad.

THE FBI BUILDING.
The J. Edgar Hoover Federal Bureau of Investigation Building (FBI Headquarters), located on Pennsylvania Avenue, opened in 1975. The building houses the famed investigative agency's records, laboratories, and administrative offices.

(ABOVE)
THE FBI FIREARMS DEMONSTRATION RANGE.
One of the most popular tourist stops is the Federal Bureau of Investigation's firearms demonstration range. The exhibits of the FBI showcase the Bureau's long and storied investigations against criminal kingpins and spies.

(OPPOSITE LEFT)
THE INTERNATIONAL SPY MUSEUM.
The International Spy Museum is one of Washington's newest museums, dedicated to telling the story of espionage from the past to the present.

(OPPOSITE RIGHT)
ARTIFACTS FROM THE INTERNATIONAL SPY MUSEUM.
Above are pistols used in the clandestine work of spies: a ring with a hidden pistol; a lipstick-pistol device; and a watch cleverly adapted to serve as a pistol. Below, is the "Enigma Machine" used by Nazi Germany to encrypt messages during World War II.

(LEFT)

INSIDE THE OCTAGON.
The interior of the Octagon, one of Washington's splendid historic homes, is a showcase of period furniture from the early days of the nation's capital.

(RIGHT TOP)

THE OCTAGON.
One of Washington's most elegant residences, the Octagon was built in the 1790s by John Taylor, a friend of George Washington. Despite its name, the Octagon has only six sides.

(RIGHT BOTTOM)

THE NATIONAL BUILDING MUSEUM.
A detail of the National Building Museum (the old Pension Building), regarded today as a venerable landmark in Washington, D.C. The old Pension building (1882–1887) was once considered an architectural oddity, derided as "Meig's Old Red Barn" after its controversial architect, Montgomery C. Meigs. For decades, pensions for the GAR (Grand Army of the Republic) veterans were processed in this historic structure.

(OPPOSITE)

INSIDE THE NATIONAL BUILDING MUSEUM.
The cavernous interior of the National Building Museum, with its extraordinary 75-foot-high Corinthian columns, has been a popular spot for presidential inaugural balls.

THE MALL

"*What is a city, but the people?*"

— WILLIAM SHAKESPEARE

THE LINCOLN MEMORIAL AND THE WASHINGTON MONUMENT.
The Mall extends from the Lincoln Memorial on the Potomac River, past the Washington Monument, to the Capitol in the distance.

THE LINCOLN MEMORIAL.
In describing his sculpture of Abraham Lincoln, Daniel Chester French said, "The Memorial tells you just what manner of man you are coming to pay homage to—his simplicity, his grandeur, and his power."

(ABOVE AND RIGHT)
THE NATIONAL WORLD WAR II MEMORIAL.
The National World War II Memorial was dedicated on May 30, 2004, on the eve of Memorial Day. A granite plaza is flanked by two arches, which represent the Atlantic and Pacific theaters of the war. The memorial, designed by architect Friedrich St. Florian, honors 16 million veterans and more than 400,000 members of the armed forces who died in the war.

(OPPOSITE)
AN AERIAL VIEW OF THE MALL.
A modern aerial perspective of the Mall showing the vast sweep and grandeur of the public space selected by Pierre L'Enfant to be the core of the new "Federal City."

Washington boasts a spacious park at its core, what Thomas Jefferson called the "Public Walk" and what we know today as the Mall. After two centuries of development, the Mall plays a lively role in American life. The rich ensemble of museums, gardens, and cultural institutions that hug the perimeter of the Mall attracts millions of tourists each year. The Mall provides a special ground for presidential memorials and monuments, offering tributes in granite and stone to George Washington, Abraham Lincoln, Thomas Jefferson, and, most recently, Franklin Delano Roosevelt. America's wars are memorialized here, including the Korean War, Vietnam War, and World War II. The Mall remains a powerful magnet for free assembly, protest, and public advocacy in a democratic society. Administered by the National Park Service, the Mall offers a congenial spot for leisurely walks and jogging, kite flying, folklife festivals, baseball games, concerts, and family outings. The annual July 4th celebration attracts hundreds of thousands of people to this epicenter of American life.

The grandeur and beauty of today's Mall stands in sharp contrast to earlier times when the open area was a rustic backwater, for many nothing short of a national embarrassment. Pierre L'Enfant's vision for the Mall had been a grand avenue extending from the Capitol to the present site of the Washington Monument. This grandiose plan never materialized. Instead, the Mall area remained largely undeveloped, except for the construction of the original Smithsonian building, affectionately known as the "Castle," in 1848. During much of the nineteenth century the Pennsylvania Railroad operated a smoke-filled train station situated on the Mall, in the very shadow of Capitol Hill. Nearby were houses, rundown buildings, and shacks clustered at one end of the Mall. Rubbish heaps, vegetable patches, grazing cows, a polluted canal, and a warren of tree-lined passageways gave the Mall a chaotic character. Marshland along the Potomac River served as the western border for this rustic strip of land.

In 1901, in a bold move by Congress to eliminate this national eyesore, Senator James McMillan of Michigan led a joint commission to transform the Mall into a beautiful park. McMillan expressed profound admiration for the original plan of L'Enfant, in particular his vision of an open and uninterrupted green space

between the Capitol and the Potomac River. Soon the McMillan commission sparked dramatic changes on the Mall. The old train station was relocated behind the Capitol, to become the impressive Union Station. Derelict houses were razed. The mounds of rubbish were cleared. The old canal and much of the marshland were systematically drained and filled in, providing sites for the eventual construction of the Lincoln and Jefferson memorials. The old dream of the Mall as the grand core precinct of L'Enfant's planned city soon became a reality. The drive to develop the Mall continues into the twenty-first century with new memorials and museums, most notably the addition of the World War II Memorial and the Smithsonian's National Museum of the American Indian.

The stately Lincoln Memorial stands at the western edge of the Mall as the nation's tribute to Abraham Lincoln, sixteenth president of the United States. With its thirty-six Doric columns and classical lines, the structure is reminiscent of the Greek Parthenon. Designed by Henry Bacon, the Lincoln Memorial was built on reclaimed marshland, opening to the public in 1922. At the center of the memorial is the famed marble statue

of a seated Lincoln, crafted by Daniel Chester French. Chiseled into the interior walls of the building are Lincoln's eloquent words contained in the Gettysburg Address and his Second Inaugural address. The Lincoln Memorial, over the decades, has emerged as a powerful symbol of American democratic values and a platform for public protest, most notably in 1963 when Martin Luther King, Jr., made his famous "I Have a Dream" speech before a crowd of 200,000 people.

As early as 1783, the Continental Congress had called for the erection of an equestrian statue to honor George Washington, the heroic leader of the American Revolution. When L'Enfant laid out his plan for the Mall, he echoed this same idea, calling for a statue to be placed in the center of the Mall—where the east-west axis from Capitol Hill intersected the north-south axis emanating from the White House. L'Enfant thought in terms of an equestrian statue as an appropriate way to honor the soldier, statesman, and founding father of the United States.

However, decades passed without any concrete plans to erect a monument to George Washington. Finally, in 1833, the Washington National Monument Society organized a campaign to

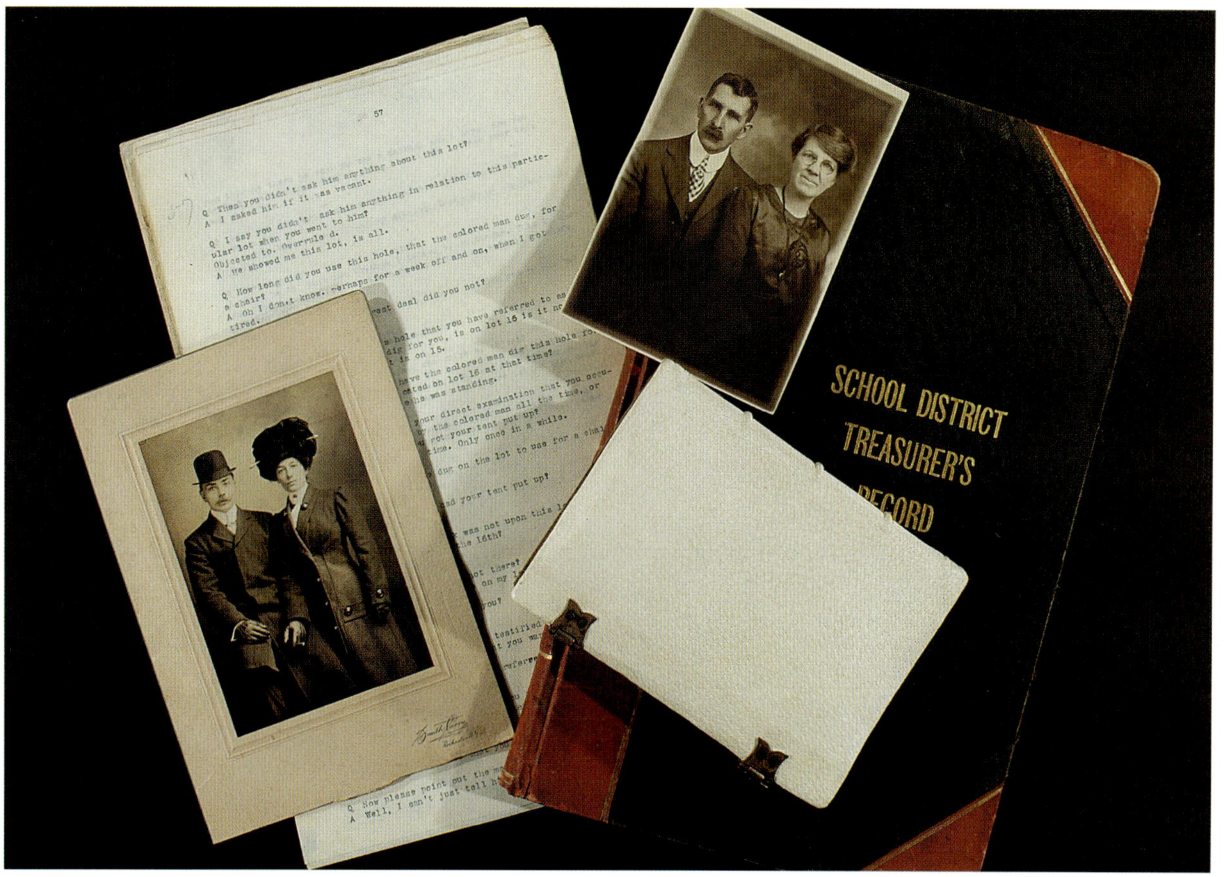

THE NATIONAL ARCHIVES.
Designed by architect John Russell Pope, the National Archives is a massive limestone structure occupying an entire city block on Constitution Avenue at the northern edge of the Mall.

(ABOVE)
FAMILY GENEALOGY.
The National Archives is a vast repository of public records, a rich source of information on family genealogy.

(LEFT)
THE DECLARATION OF INDEPENDENCE, THE CONSTITUTION, AND THE BILL OF RIGHTS.
Also at the National Archives, visitors may see up close the Declaration of Independence and fragments of the Constitution and Bill of Rights—the very instruments of American democracy.

THE SMITHSONIAN
INSTITUTION GARDENS.
*The elegant Enid A. Haupt
Garden of the Smithsonian
Institution occupies the south
lawn of the Smithsonian
complex, with walkways*
*to the Castle (the main
Smithsonian building) and
nearby museums dedicated to
African and Asian art.*

THE SMITHSONIAN
INSTITUTION.
*The Smithsonian Institution
building, affectionately known
as the "Castle," viewed in
silhouette on the Mall. The red
sandstone structure, designed*
*by architect James Renwick,
opened in 1855. Today, the
Castle is at the epicenter of the
Smithsonian's art, history, and
science museums.*

raise the necessary funds for a Washington monument. The idea of an obelisk eventually won out over rival plans for a memorial. Fund-raising proved to be uneven and sporadic, slowing work on the monument. During the years of the Civil War, 1861–1865, all work on the monument ceased because of the war emergency. For many years, only a rump version of the stone monument was visible on the Mall, an ugly and embarrassing reminder of an ill-fated, if noble, project to memorialize the first president. Finally, with the aid of Congress, the Washington Monument was completed and dedicated on February 21, 1885. Today, the 555-foot Washington Monument dominates the Mall, offering a signature image of the nation's capital.

The Castle (the Smithsonian Institution Building), designed by James Renwick and built of red sandstone, occupies a central place in the Mall—as both the image and administrative heart of the Smithsonian Institution. Initially financed by a bequest of James Smithson (1765–1829), the Smithsonian Institution has evolved into the world's largest complex of museums and research organizations—dedicated to "the increase and diffusion of knowledge," the original mandate

given to the Smithsonian by its namesake and benefactor. The distinctive Castle building reflects Renwick's artistry; he designed the building in the spirit of the Gothic revival of the mid-nineteenth century. Today, the old Smithsonian Building survives intact but now incorporates a number of changes in its Quadrangle Museums Project, including the Enid A. Haupt Garden complex, the underground S. Dillon Ripley Center, and the addition of two museums, also underground, the Sackler Gallery for Asian Art and the National Museum of African Art.

The rich legacy of American history, science, and culture is preserved in the Smithsonian complex of museums. The National Museum of American History with its millions of artifacts and interpretive exhibits contains within its walls some highly popular national treasures such as the Star-Spangled Banner and first ladies' inaugural gowns.

Across the Mall is the Smithsonian National Air and Space Museum. Containing a unique collection of aerospace artifacts, the museum showcases some memorable flying machines that altered the course of history: the first successful airplane, the 1903 Wright Brothers Flyer, Charles

Lindbergh's *Spirit of St. Louis*, remembered for the first solo crossing of the Atlantic in 1927, and the Apollo 11 capsule that carried astronauts to the Moon in 1969, among many others.

The National Archives, a large limestone structure situated on the northern edge of the Mall between Constitution and Pennsylvania avenues, rivals the Smithsonian museums with its historical artifacts and documents. Designed by John Russell Pope, the huge rectangular National Archives building evokes an imposing and awe-inspiring presence on the Mall, occupying an entire city block. Visitors entering the building from the Constitution Avenue side encounter the famed Rotunda (often called the Shrine), which contains the "Charters of Freedom," consisting of the Declaration of Independence, pages from the Constitution, and the Bill of Rights.

Nearby, one of America's most famous art galleries, the National Gallery of Art, contains a superlative collection of masterpieces, covering the period from the thirteenth century to the present. John Russell Pope designed the domed west wing of the National Gallery of Art complex. Inspired by the classical revival style, the windowless west building is adorned with a pink Tennessee marble façade. Financier and industrialist Andrew Mellon (1855–1937) endowed the National Gallery of Art with financial support and his own rich art collection; other donors followed with contributions of art to make the National Gallery one of the preeminent art museums in the world.

With its ever-expanding art collections and lively exhibitions, the National Gallery opened a new addition in 1978 called the East Wing. The new addition represented a sharp departure from the neo-classical lines of the parent building, offering visitors to the Mall a radically modern design by architect I. M. Pei. Often considered an art object in its own right, the East Wing, consisting of two separate, overlapping triangles, is built on a trapezoidal site at the intersection of Constitution and Pennsylvania avenues. The marble for the East Wing was mined from the same quarry that provided the façade for the old building, assuring a sense of harmony between the two wings of the National Gallery of Art. The Mall also boasts two sculpture gardens, the National Gallery of Art Sculpture Garden (with an operating ice rink in the winter months) and the Smithsonian's counterpart, the Hirshhorn Museum's ensemble of twentieth-century sculpture set in a subterranean garden plot.

Juxtaposed to the art museums are the many war memorials on the Mall. The moving simplicity of the Vietnam Veterans Memorial (completed in 1982), designed by architect Maya Ying Lin, has attracted millions of visitors. Lin won the national design competition for the memorial while still an undergraduate at Yale University. The names of over 58,000 Vietnam War dead are inscribed on the black marble wall of the memorial, augmented with three-dimensional statuary—the *Three Servicemen Statue* and the *Vietnam Women's Memorial*. The sacrifice of Americans in the Korean War and World War II are also immortalized on the Mall.

The United States Holocaust Memorial Museum represents a powerful and moving tribute to victims of another tragedy of the twentieth century, the systematic persecution and annihilation of European Jews and other minorities by Nazi Germany in the years 1933–1945. Located near the Mall on 14th Street, the United States Holocaust Memorial Museum offers unique exhibits and research facilities for the study of the Holocaust.

The Mall remains a public park devoted to art, culture, science, and historical memory.

(LEFT TOP)
EAST WING OF THE NATIONAL GALLERY OF ART.
Alexander Calder's mobile Untitled (1976) moves serenely above the central atrium in the East Building at the National Gallery of Art.

(LEFT BOTTOM)
AN AERIAL VIEW OF THE NATIONAL GALLERY OF ART.
Designed by architect I. M. Pei, the East Building at the National Gallery of Art occupies an odd trapezoidal slice of land on the Mall, just below Capitol Hill. The unusual design offers a sharp contrast to the more classical lines of the neighboring West Building.

(RIGHT)
THE WEST BUILDING OF THE NATIONAL GALLERY OF ART.
The striking rotunda of the National Gallery of Art is fashioned with a central fountain and sculpture of Mercury surrounded by a double circle of sixteen Italian marble columns.

(RIGHT TOP)

THE HIRSHHORN MUSEUM. *Called the "concrete donut" by some critics, the Joseph H. Hirshhorn Museum is part of the complex of Smithsonian art museums, housing a world-renowned collection of modernist art. Designed by Gordon Bunshaft (1909–1990), the Hirshhorn contains important masterpieces of twentieth-century artists from Pablo Picasso to Andy Warhol. Adjacent to the Hirshhorn building is a 1.3-acre Sculpture Garden.*

(RIGHT BOTTOM)

THE SCULPTURE GARDEN AT THE HIRSHHORN MUSEUM. *The "Nymph" statue in the Sculpture Garden of the Hirshhorn Museum, located on the Mall.*

(LEFT)

THE NATIONAL AIR AND SPACE MUSEUM SPACE HALL.
Space Hall at the Smithsonian National Air and Space Museum is a spacious exhibit hall dedicated to the history of rocketry and space exploration. The huge exhibit area contains a variety of rockets, satellites, and space artifacts, including the Apollo-Soyuz capsules.

(ABOVE)

THE HAZY CENTER.
The Steven F. Udvar-Hazy Center at Washington Dulles International Airport houses historic aircraft of the National Air and Space Museum, including the high-altitude spy plane, the SR-71, and the supersonic Concorde airliner. The popular Dulles center opened on the occasion of the Centennial of Flight in December 2003.

(OPPOSITE)

MILESTONES OF FLIGHT GALLERY.
The Milestones of Flight Gallery occupies a central place in the National Air and Space Museum. The 1903 Wright Flyer soars above the gallery. Around the Wright flying machine are numerous historic artifacts, including Charles Lindbergh's Spirit of St. Louis and the Apollo 11 capsule.

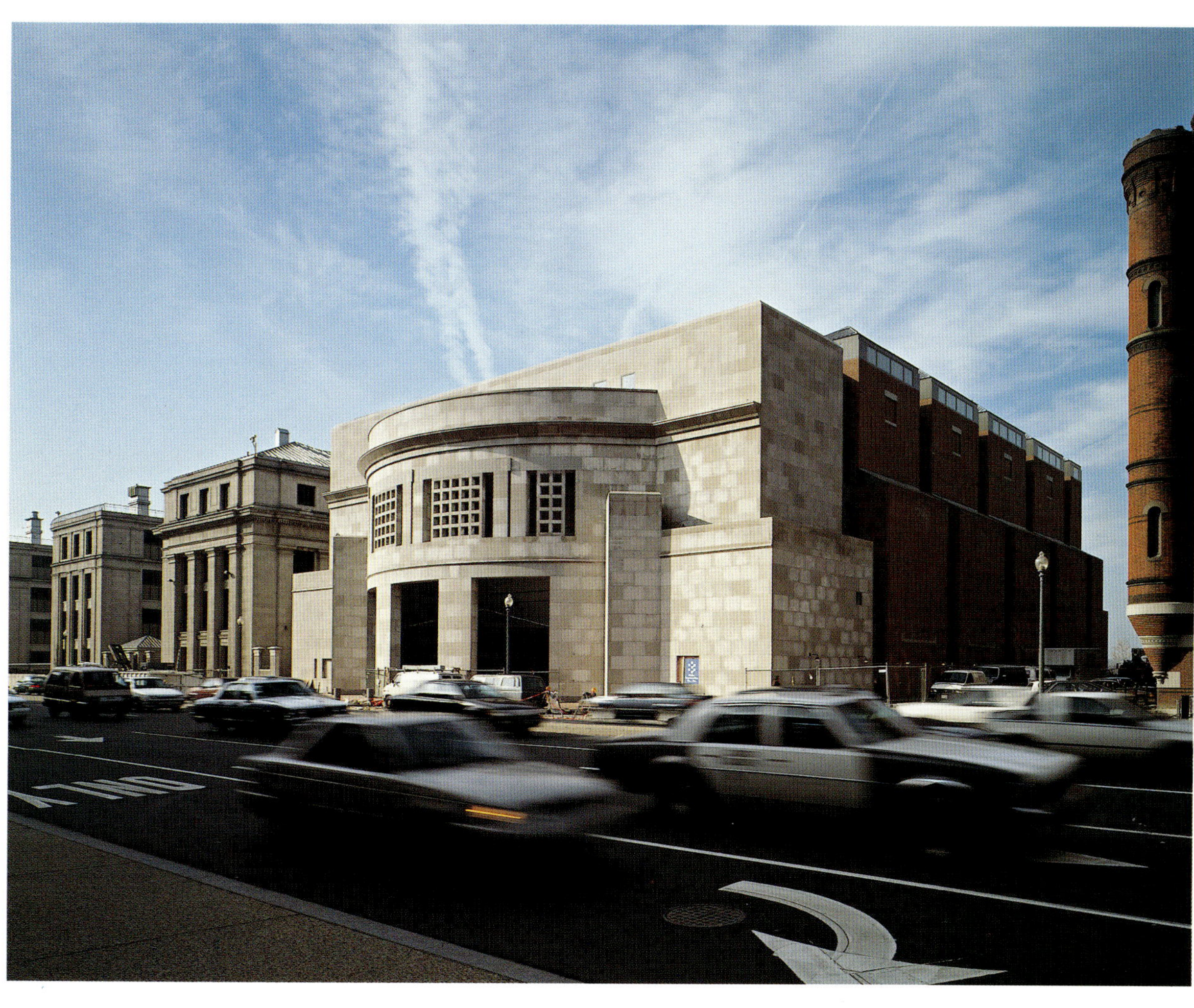

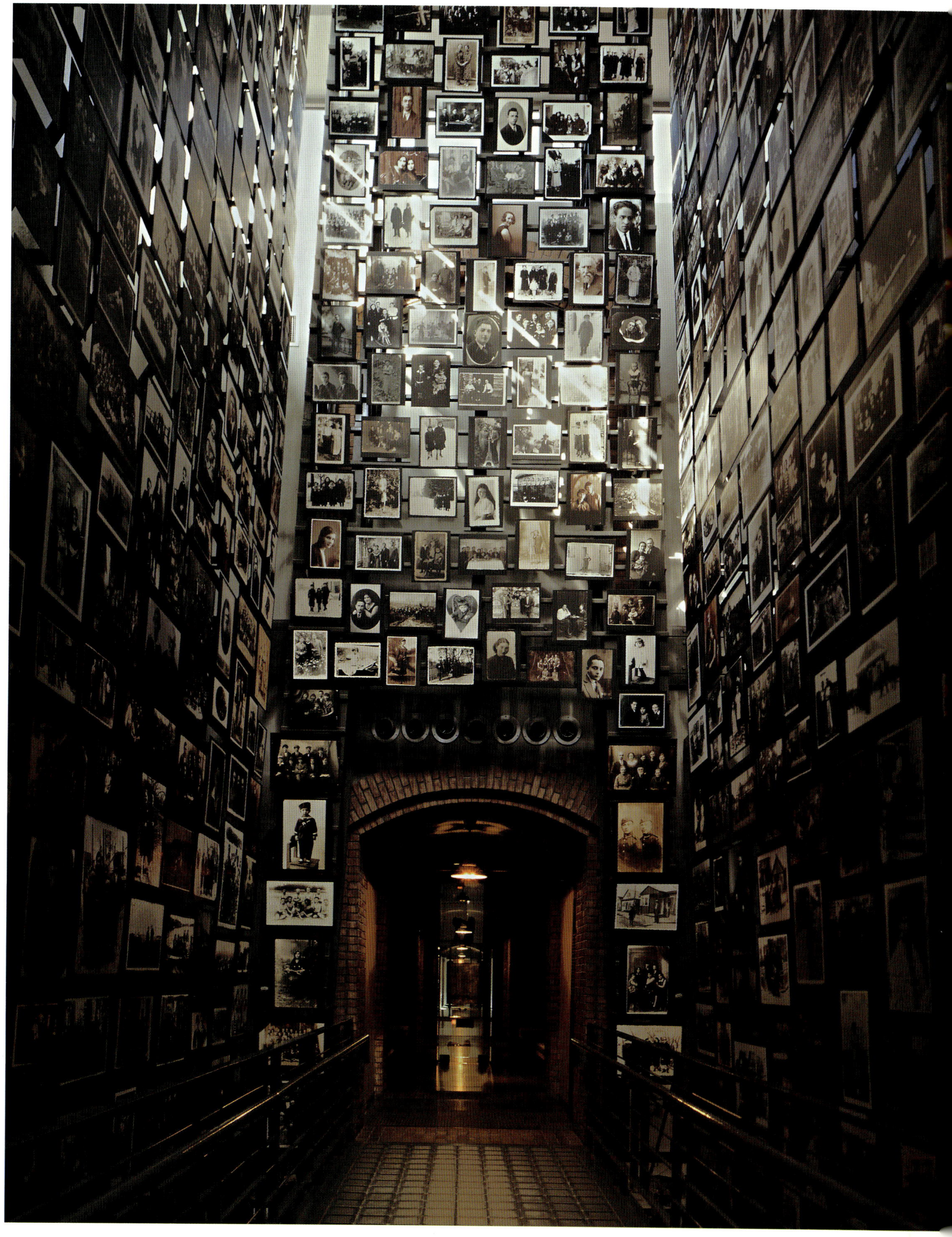

(OPPOSITE)
INSIDE THE UNITED STATES HOLOCAUST MEMORIAL MUSEUM.
The United States Holocaust Memorial Museum is located just off the Mall between 14th Street and Raoul Wallenberg Place. Shown in this photograph is the front of a railway car used to transport victims of the Holocaust to the death camps.

(ABOVE)
THE UNITED STATES HOLOCAUST MEMORIAL MUSEUM.
The United States Holocaust Memorial Museum was designed by James Ingo Freed and opened in 1993.

(RIGHT)
THE HALL OF PORTRAITS AT THE UNITED STATES HOLOCAUST MEMORIAL MUSEUM.
One Holocaust Museum exhibit displays the photographs of victims from one town in Poland caught up in the Nazi Party's campaign of repression that led to the death of more than 6 million European Jews.

(LEFT)

THE FDR WATERFALL.
The waterfall at the Franklin Delano Roosevelt Memorial is located near the Tidal Basin at the west end of the Mall, within short walking distance of the other major presidential memorials dedicated to Thomas Jefferson and Abraham Lincoln.

(ABOVE)

THE FDR MEMORIAL.
The Franklin Delano Roosevelt Memorial, completed in 1997, shows the thirty-second president with his beloved Scottie, Fala. Roosevelt is memorialized as the president who led the nation during the Great Depression and World War II.

(OPPOSITE)

THE FDR MEMORIAL AT NIGHT.
Designed by Lawrence Halprin, the FDR Memorial consists of granite walls with four outdoor rooms, each linked to a particular theme associated with the Roosevelt presidency.

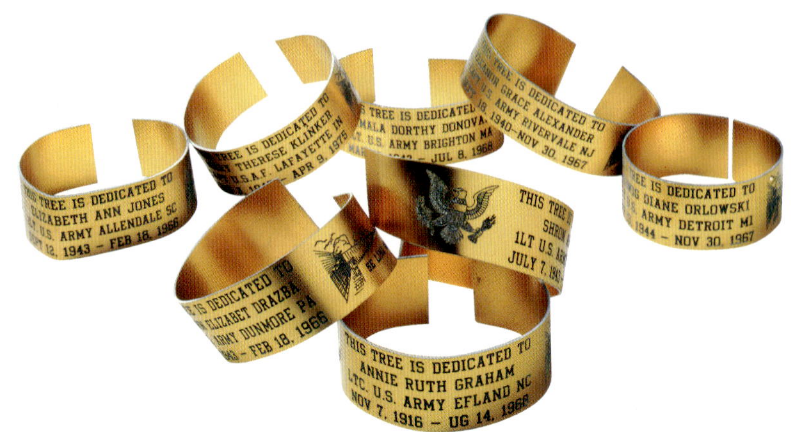

(FAR LEFT)
THE VIETNAM VETERANS MEMORIAL.
Maya Ying Lin's moving tribute to the men and women who died in the Vietnam War. Dedicated in 1983, the memorial includes the names of more than 58,000 dead etched in black granite.

(ABOVE)
ARTIFACTS FROM THE VIETNAM WAR.
Symbolic bracelets of nurses killed in the Vietnam War.

(LEFT TOP)
VIETNAM VETERANS NURSES MEMORIAL.
The Vietnam Veterans Memorial also contains this tribute to the women who participated in the Vietnam conflict. The sculpture, designed by Glenna Goodacre, depicts three women attending to a wounded soldier.

(LEFT BOTTOM)
A RUBBING FROM THE MEMORIAL WALL.
A veteran makes a charcoal rubbing of a name from the wall of the Vietnam Veterans Memorial. Few places on the Mall possess the compelling appeal of this war memorial.

(RIGHT)
FOURTH OF JULY CELEBRATION IN WASHINGTON.
The Washington Monument is illuminated by a massive fireworks display on a fourth of July Independence Day celebration.

THE AVENUES

"Ah, to build, to build!
That is the noblest of all the arts."
– HENRY WADSWORTH LONGFELLOW

(FOLDOUT)
THE WHITE HOUSE ELLIPSE.
The Ellipse behind the White House offers a grand setting for state visits and other public ceremonies. The Ellipse fronts on the Mall, offering a dramatic view of the White House from Constitution Avenue.

(PANORAMA)
THE WHITE HOUSE.
The White House, located at 1600 Pennsylvania Avenue, mirrors the 1792 design by architect James Hoban. First occupied by the nation's second president, John Adams and his wife, Abigail Adams, the White House was nearly destroyed in 1814 in a raid by the British. Rebuilt and subject to numerous renovations and additions, the White House is a powerful symbol of the American presidency.

When Pierre L'Enfant laid out his plan for Washington, he proposed an elaborate grid of streets, intersected by broad avenues with "round points" or circles. The designated circles, by design, were intended to serve as the foci for new neighborhoods. Separate from his rational street grid, L'Enfant's plan called for a "Grand Avenue," a projected 400-foot-wide thoroughfare below Capitol Hill lined with embassies and public buildings with a towering equestrian statue of George Washington.

This proposed scheme never materialized; over time, this expansive open area leading to the Potomac River became the Mall. However, other key elements in L'Enfant's geometry for a planned city did come to fruition: the mile-long corridor from Capitol Hill to the White House (present-day Pennsylvania Avenue) quickly evolved into the most prominent boulevard in Washington. This celebrated avenue and the Mall became the core for L'Enfant's plan.

Washington in time acquired a well-deserved reputation for being "the city of magnificent distances." Along the wide avenues of the city there arose monumental public buildings and museums, memorials, churches, parks, and grand houses. Avenues radiating out from the Capitol were often named for the states of the Union, a gesture to express the organic links of the Federal City to the nation at large.

Old and new architecture often co-exist on the avenues of Washington, D.C. The celebrated Pennsylvania Avenue, for example, has undergone more than one transformation over the decades, reflecting changing tastes in architecture and the ever-expanding need for public buildings. When President John F. Kennedy rode from the Capitol to the White House on his inauguration day in 1961, Pennsylvania Avenue was a derelict corridor of pawnshops, bars, liquor stores, and secondhand shops—with no residential buildings surviving. The so-called Avenue of Presidents was closed at dark, except for a hotel, a restaurant, and Apex Liquors at 7th Street, the venerable old structure that once was home to Mathew Brady's photography studio, where Abraham Lincoln sat for his last portrait.

Later President Kennedy appointed Arthur Goldberg, his secretary of labor, to head the Council on Pennsylvania Avenue. Daniel Patrick Moynihan, later senator from New York, played a key role in the creative work of the committee to transform the historic street, to fashion a "living

(LEFT)

THE NATIONAL CHRISTMAS TREE.

The 2001 Christmas season is celebrated on the White House grounds with a large and festive Christmas tree, shown here illuminated at night with the White House in the distance.

(BELOW)

THE OVAL OFFICE.

The Oval Office in the "West Wing" of the White House is the private office of American presidents and is a symbol of executive power and the hub of U.S. policy making. Much of American history intersects in this famous office space.

(LEFT)
THE WHITE HOUSE GREEN ROOM.
(LEFT)
**THE WHITE HOUSE
GREEN ROOM.**
*The Green Room at the White
House has served multiple
purposes since 1800, from a
bedroom for presidential guests
to a dining room. Authentic*
*Federal-period furniture
was installed in the 1920s
during the administration
of Calvin Coolidge.*

(OPPOSITE LEFT)
**THE WHITE HOUSE
RED ROOM.**
*This small parlor room known
as the "Red Room" is enhanced
with its gilded furniture,
antiques, and a bust of*
*President Martin Van Buren.
Eleanor Roosevelt used the
room in the 1930s for meetings
with women reporters.*

downtown." Kennedy's initiative suggested how one president (with the assistance of First Lady Jacqueline Kennedy) could stimulate urban renewal, even though in earlier years Congress had played a major role in shaping the character of the city. The renewal of Pennsylvania Avenue evolved as a careful blend of old and new: today, modern designs such as I. M. Pei's stunning East Wing of the National Gallery of Art share the famous avenue with renovated historic structures, most notably the Old Post Office and the Willard Hotel.

The White House, located at 1600 Pennsylvania Avenue, has been the official home of American presidents since the administration of Thomas Jefferson. Designed by an Irishman, James Hoban, and constructed of Virginia sandstone painted white, the president's mansion is the oldest public building in the District of Columbia, the cornerstone having been laid on October 13, 1792. Thomas Jefferson played a key role in shaping the original design of the White House and, as the first occupant, he personally oversaw the creation of nearby Lafayette Square and the landscaping for the new "President's Park" (White House grounds), adding a circular drive and terraces. Never fully pleased with the executive mansion, Jefferson once complained that

the structure was "big enough for two emperors, one Pope, and the Grand Lama." His successors, however, viewed the structure as an architectural masterpiece, a fitting symbol of the American presidency.

The White House, by circumstance or design, underwent several renovations in the centuries that followed. Nearly destroyed by the British in August 1814, the structure had to be rebuilt during the administration of James Madison. Other, less dramatic, renovations came with the passing of time: Andrew Jackson added running water; Franklin Pierce devised a system for central heating; Rutherford Hayes installed the first bathroom; James Garfield arranged for the construction of the first elevator; Herbert Hoover initiated the design of the first air conditioning system; Harry Truman added a second-story porch; and First Lady Jacqueline Kennedy sought out historic American furniture and antiques for the interior of the White House. In modern times, most presidents with their first ladies felt compelled to engage in some form of redecoration, a conscious desire to leave their own imprint on the venerable residence.

The international character of the city is enshrined on "Embassy Row," a two-mile stretch of Massachusetts Avenue between Scott Circle and

(ABOVE)

THE WHITE HOUSE STATE DINING ROOM.
Decorated in gold and white, the State Dining Room reflects the ambience of an eighteenth-century English home. The dining room can accommodate up to 140 people for state occasions.

(LEFT)

THE WHITE HOUSE BLUE ROOM.
The elliptical "Blue Room" includes French Empire-style furniture and a gilded wood chandelier. Used as a reception area, the Blue Room also contains paintings of American presidents.

THE KOREAN WAR VETERANS MEMORIAL.
The open-air memorial to the Korean War located on the Mall takes on a somber reality with snow-covered statues of American soldiers replicating the image of the harsh conditions associated with the Korean conflict (1950–1953).

THE CIVIL WAR FRIEZE.
The National Building Museum (the old Pension Building) is decorated with an extraordinary frieze honoring the many battles and military triumphs of the Union Army in the Civil War.

Observatory Circle. This section of the avenue was once lined with many upscale private residences, designed in the Beaux-Arts style popular at the turn of the twentieth century. Wealthy tycoons, using fortunes earned in publishing, railroads, banking, and other pursuits, built stately homes on or near Massachusetts Avenue, creating what some have called Washington's *belle époque.* By the 1930s, however, the area began to be transformed into a distinct diplomatic quarter, a shift sparked by the governments of Great Britain and Japan purchasing elegant homes to serve as their embassy compounds. Today, Massachusetts Avenue is home to many diplomatic missions, a corridor festooned with the colorful flags of numerous nations.

The fifty-room Walsh-McLean house, just above Dupont Circle, currently houses the embassy of Indonesia. Once the palatial home of Thomas F. Walsh, the house was constructed in 1903 at a cost of $835,000—at the time an astronomical figure. Designed by Danish-born architect Henry Anderson, the house reflects more than an architectural style, with the interior marked by a curved Art Nouveau mahogany balustrade. In contrast to the flamboyant Walsh-McLean house is the Japanese embassy,

constructed in 1932 in the Georgian revival style.

Some of Washington's most elegant homes have been transformed into museums. One famous example is Hillwood, a neo-Georgian mansion located on Linnean Avenue above Rock Creek Park and once the home of eccentric cereal heiress Marjorie Merriweather Post. Hillwood now houses a rare collection of Russian antiques, icons, and art, including celebrated Fabergé eggs. Many of Hillwood's precious tsarist-era artifacts were confiscated from churches and private owners in Russia and then sold to Post's third husband, Joseph E. Davies, who served as United States ambassador to the Soviet Union in the late 1930s.

The avenues of Washington boast many houses of worship. Washington National Cathedral (technically the Cathedral Church of St. Peter and St. Paul), perhaps the best known house of worship, is situated on Wisconsin Avenue on a 57-acre site dubbed Mount St. Alban, one of the most elevated spots in the District of Columbia. Known as one of the most beautiful examples of English Gothic design, Washington Cathedral is administered by the Episcopal Church. Construction of the cathedral took 83 years, reaching completion in September 1990. The intent of the cathedral has been to serve as

Augustus Saint-Gaudens sculpted the haunting statue in the Rock Creek Cemetery at the Adams Memorial to Marian Adams. Titled The Peace of God that Passeth Understanding, *it is often erroneously called "Grief."*

"a great church for national purposes," and often the place for state funerals and memorials. President Theodore Roosevelt laid the cornerstone in 1907, and the cathedral has played a visible role in American life over the decades of its existence. Built with Indiana limestone, the National Cathedral is awe-inspiring with its flying buttresses, vaulted interior, stained glass windows, gargoyles, and towers.

Washington's other major cathedral is the Roman Catholic National Shrine of the Immaculate Conception, located at 4th Street and Michigan Avenue. A harmonious mix of Byzantine and Romanesque architectural styles, the National Shrine has a massive dome of 108 feet, adorned with gold leaf and blue, gold, and red tiles. Towering above the complex is the Knights of Columbus Bell Tower, standing 329 feet and containing a carillon of 56 bells. The stunning interior of the church contains many mosaics, side chapels, and some 200 windows.

Many diverse religious groups have selected the Washington Metropolitan area to construct houses of worship. Among these structures, perhaps the Islamic Center on Massachusetts Avenue and the Mormon Temple in Kensington, Maryland, are the most outstanding. The Islamic Center, built by

Egyptians, is a beautiful mosque constructed of white limestone with verses from the Koran placed on the entrance. The Mormon Temple stands astride the bustling Washington Beltway near Kensington, Maryland, with its towering spire of 288 feet. The exotic appearance of the Temple has prompted some irreverent commuters on the Beltway to refer to the familiar landmark as "Oz."

The avenues of Washington memorialize humanity, as well as architecture. The statue of Albert Einstein (1879–1955) just off the Mall on Constitution Avenue and 23rd Street celebrates the life of one of history's most famed scientists, a theoretical physicist who made a profound impact on modern life. The black granite statue shows Einstein in a relaxed pose, holding a book. One of the most popular photo opportunities in Washington, the statue is situated on the grounds of the National Academy of Sciences. Just north of Dupont Circle, Mahatma Gandhi is memorialized in a bronze statue. The sculpture stands near the Indian embassy, a tribute to the role played by Gandhi in Indian independence. Also, the Lebanese poet Kahlil Gibran is honored in a beautiful garden in Rock Creek Park. These memorials add a human touch to the magnificent avenues of Washington, D.C.

WASHINGTON NATIONAL CATHEDRAL.
Washington National Cathedral (Cathedral of St. Peter and St. Paul) is a striking example of English Gothic architecture. The impressive cathedral is officially tied to the Episcopal Diocese of Washington but has served as a setting for public gatherings and ecumenical religious services.

FRIEZE AT WASHINGTON NATIONAL CATHEDRAL.
One of the most imaginative porticos of the Washington National Cathedral is Frederick Hart's interpretation of the Creation as a vortex of human forms emerging out of nothingness. The Washington Cathedral is a blend of traditional Gothic architectural and modern themes.

(LEFT)

INSIDE WASHINGTON NATIONAL CATHEDRAL.
The soaring Gothic interior of Washington National Cathedral.

(ABOVE)

STAINED GLASS WINDOW AT WASHINGTON NATIONAL CATHEDRAL.
Washington National Cathedral is adorned with a striking stained glass window containing a moon rock.

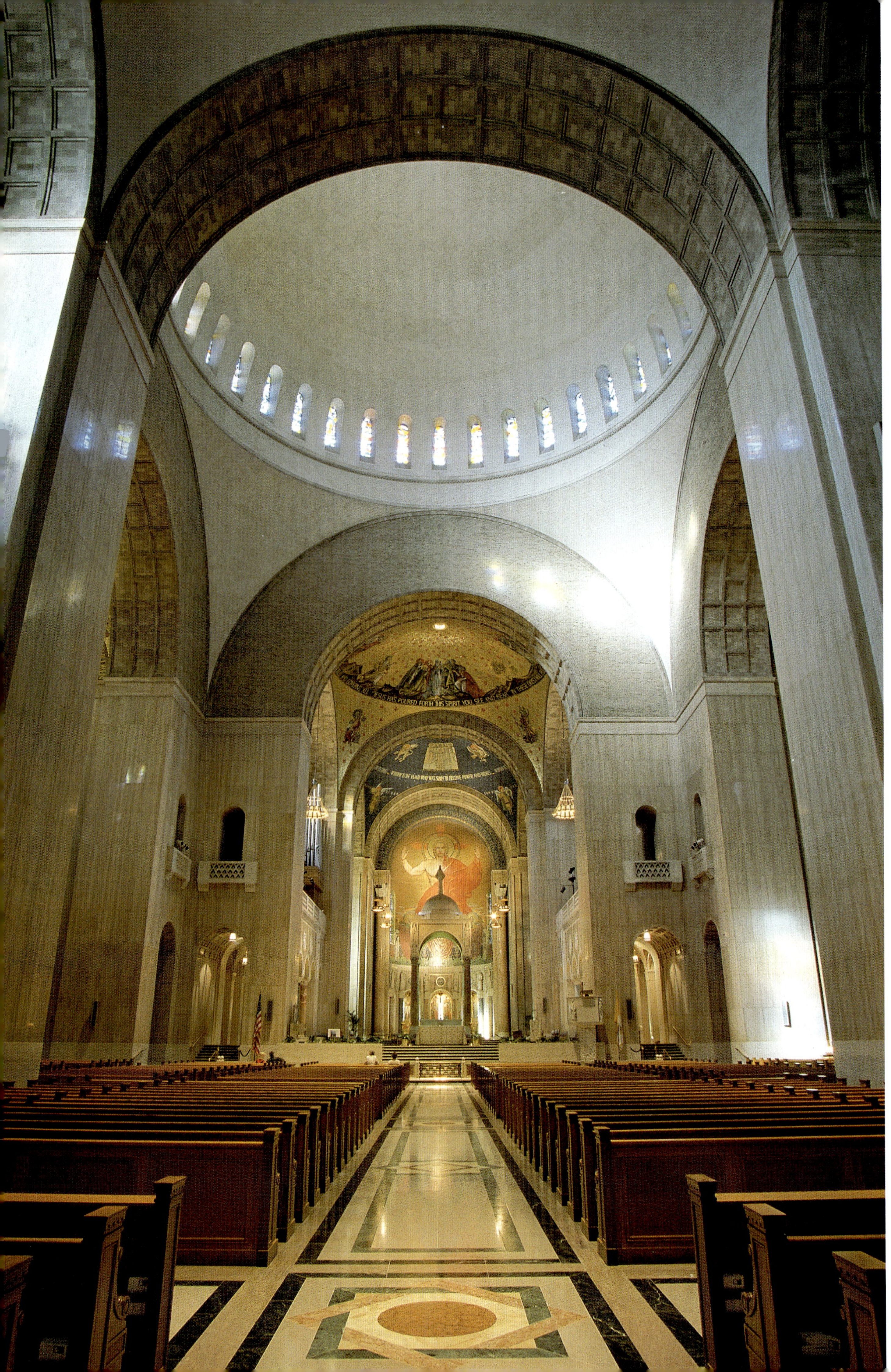

(LEFT)

Inside the Roman Catholic National Shrine.

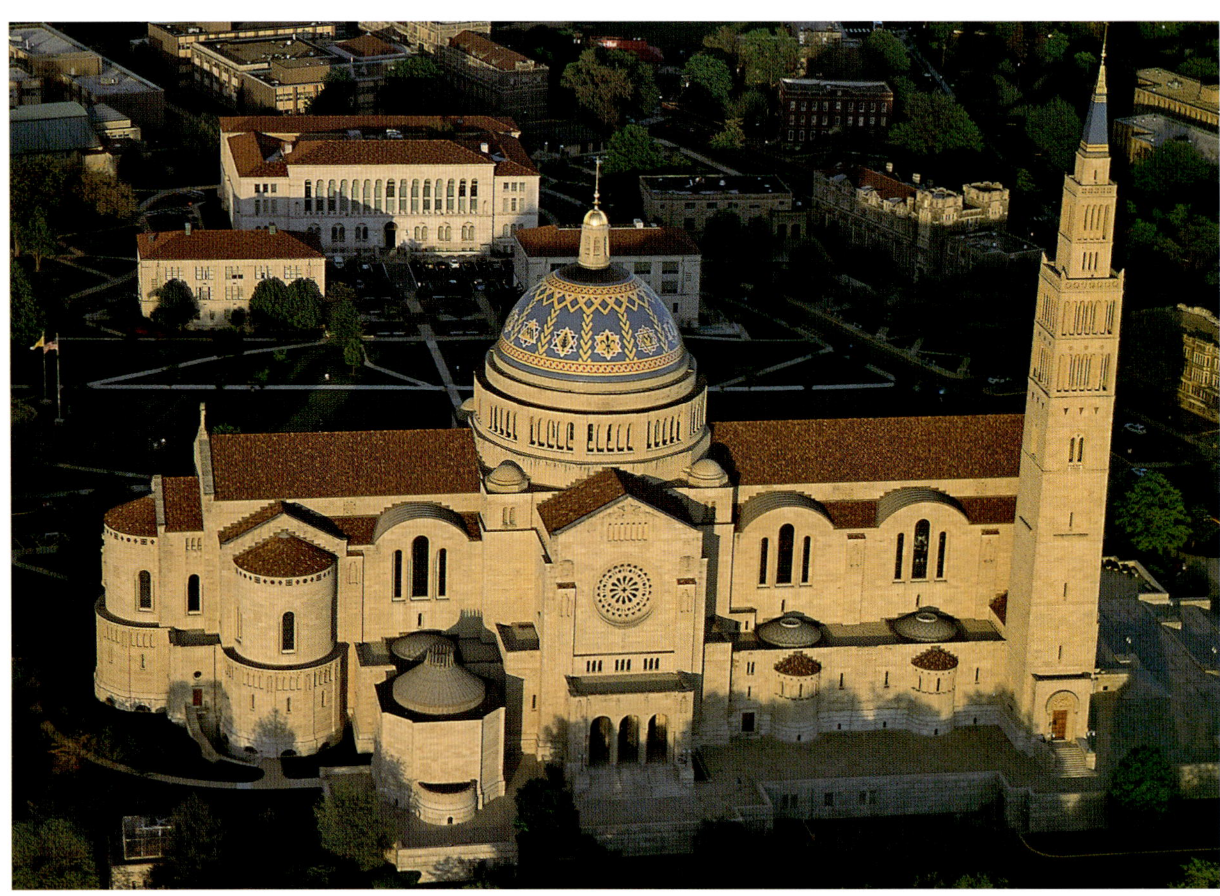

The majestic sanctuary of the Roman Catholic National Shrine of the Immaculate Conception is illuminated by some 200 windows, including three rose windows. The main altar is decorated with a mosaic portraying Christ in majesty.

(ABOVE)

The National Shrine of the Immaculate Conception.

The National Shrine of the Immaculate Conception blends Byzantine and Romanesque architectural styles. The 108-foot dome's exterior is adorned with gold leaf with blue, gold, and red tiles. The Knights' Tower (a gift of the Knights of Columbus) stands 329 feet, making the National Shrine a highly visible presence in the skyline of Washington, D.C.

(ABOVE)

THE ISLAMIC CENTER.
A distinctive white edifice on Massachusetts Avenue, the Islamic Center was built between 1949 and 1957 by Muslim countries with embassies in Washington, D.C. The mosque contains elaborate mosaics, carpets, and furniture.

(RIGHT)

THE MORMON TEMPLE.
The Mormon Temple (Church of Jesus Christ of Latter-day Saints) is located outside the District of Columbia in Kensington, Maryland. For commuters, the Temple with its exotic and soaring spires is a familiar sight on the Washington Beltway.

(LEFT)

HILLWOOD MUSEUM FABERGÉ EGG.
Among the most cherished artifacts in the Hillwood Museum are two Imperial Eggs fashioned by Fabergé in his workshop in St. Petersburg, Russia, for the Russian Imperial Court. Pictured here is the 1914 Catherine the Great Egg, presented as an Easter gift from Nicholas II to his mother, Marie Feodorovna.

(RIGHT)

HILLWOOD MUSEUM.
The interior of the Hillwood Museum echoes the lavish lifestyle of Marjorie Merriweather Post, the cereal heiress who decorated the home and later filled the house with rare Russian antiques.

(RIGHT TOP)
HILLWOOD MUSEUM.
*Hillwood, located above
Rock Creek Park, offers visitors
acres of beautiful gardens
to tour.*

(RIGHT BOTTOM)
**ICONS IN THE
HILLWOOD MUSEUM.**
*As the wife of American
ambassador to the Soviet
Union Joseph Davies, who
served from 1937 to 1938,
Marjorie Merriweather Post
was able to purchase a rich
collection of confiscated icons
and other tsarist-era antiques
from the Stalinist regime.*

(LEFT TOP)
EMBASSY ROW AND THE JAPANESE EMBASSY. *Extending from Dupont Circle, down Massachusetts Avenue to the vice president's house, Embassy Row is the location of many foreign embassies in Washington. Most of the residences are former elegant homes of wealthy inhabitants of Washington, built in the late nineteenth century and the early decades of the twentieth century. The serene interior of the Japanese embassy, one of the most beautiful foreign residences in the city, is considered a National Historic Landmark.*

(LEFT BOTTOM)
THE INDONESIAN EMBASSY. *The embassy of Indonesia occupies the former Walsh-McLean mansion. Once the private residence of mining entrepreneur Thomas Walsh, the home is a fine example of the opulent mansions built on Massachusetts Avenue at the turn of the twentieth century.*

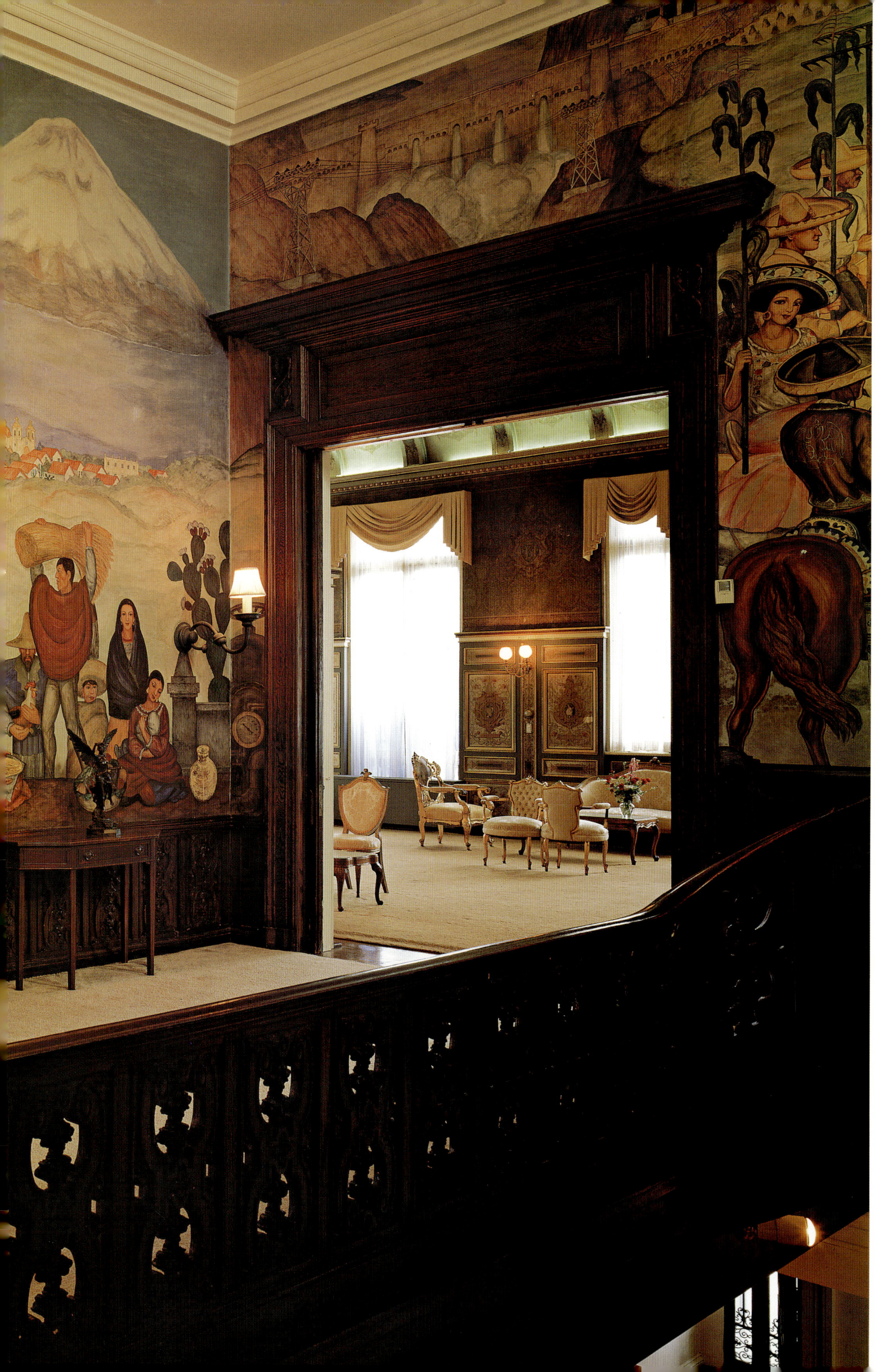

(LEFT)
THE MEXICAN EMBASSY.
The lavish interior of the embassy of Mexico.

(RIGHT)
THE SPANISH EMBASSY.
The vaulted elegance inside the Spanish embassy.

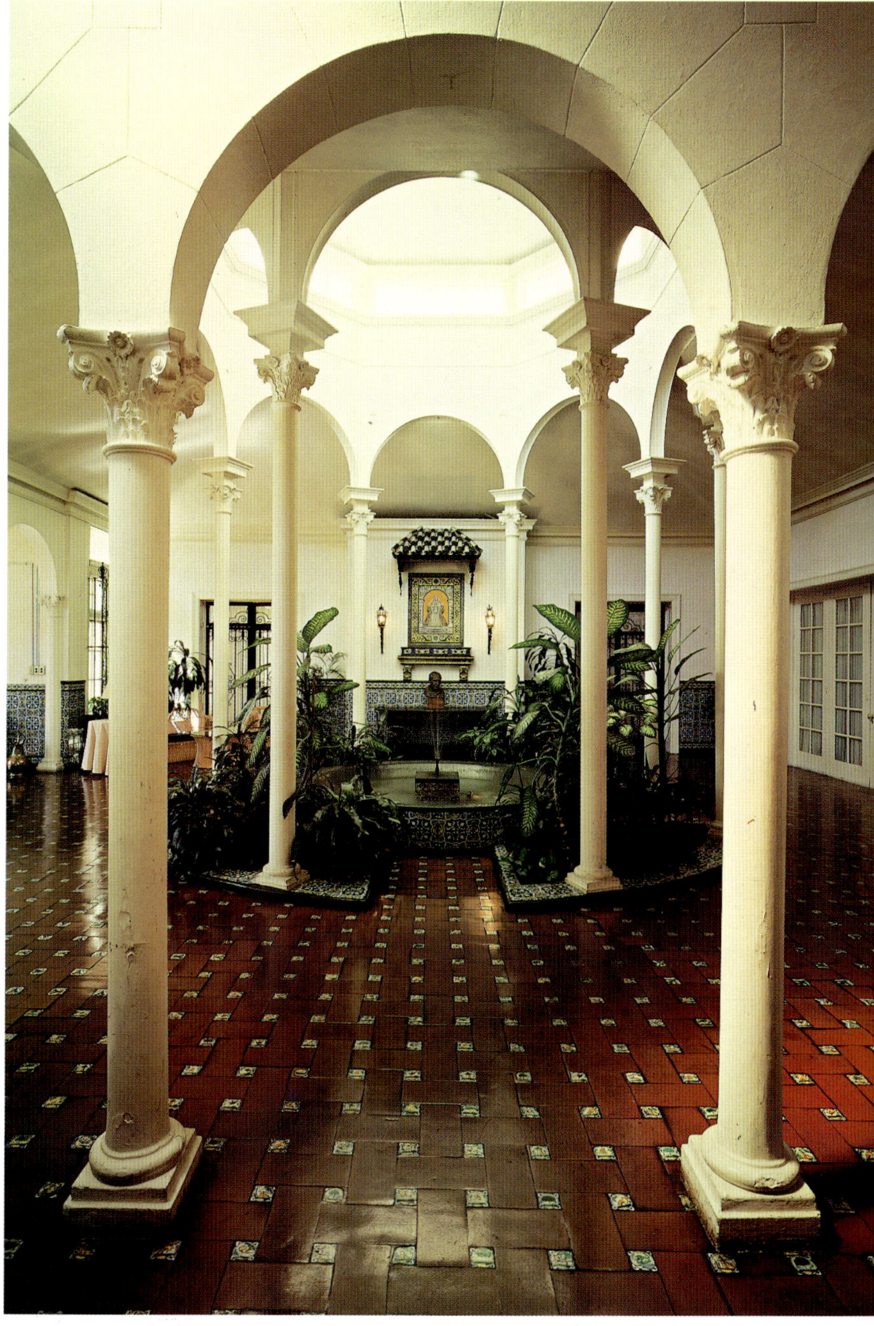

(OPPOSITE LEFT)

MAHATMA GANDHI STATUE.
Mahatma Gandhi is one of several major international leaders who are memorialized in Washington. Gandhi's statue is located across from the embassy of India, near Dupont Circle, and is a moving tribute to his life and legacy.

(OPPOSITE RIGHT)

KHALIL GIBRAN STATUE.
The Khalil Gibran Memorial recognizes the life and legacy of the Lebanese poet and religious thinker.

(LEFT)

ALBERT EINSTEIN STATUE.
The whimsical portrayal of a seated Albert Einstein by Robert Berks is a popular memorial to the famed scientist and is located at the National Academy of Sciences.

(RIGHT)

WINSTON CHURCHILL STATUE.
A statue of Winston Churchill stands in front of the British embassy on Massachusetts Avenue, portraying the famous British leader with the "V" sign for victory during World War II.

NATIONAL ZOO GIFT.
Among the most visible and popular animals at the National Zoo are the pandas, obtained from the People's Republic of China.

(RIGHT TOP)
THE NATIONAL ZOOLOGICAL PARK.
A baby elephant named Kandula was born on November 25, 2001, at the National Zoo. The male Asian elephant was given the name "Kandula" (meaning strength and virtue) after a famous elephant in Sri Lanka. The National Zoological Park is a bureau of the Smithsonian Institution and houses over 2,700 animals of 435 species inside its 63-acre Rock Creek Park complex.

(RIGHT BOTTOM)
SUMATRA TIGER.
One of the most beautiful animals in captivity at the National Zoo is the Sumatra tiger.

(OPPOSITE)
LEMURS.
Ringed-tailed lemurs huddle together, casting wary eyes toward onlookers at the National Zoo.

CAPITOL HILL

*"The American, by nature, is optimistic.
He is experimental, an inventor, and a
builder who builds best when called
upon to build greatly."*
– JOHN F. KENNEDY

When Congress finalized plans to build a new capital city on the shores of the Potomac River in 1791, President George Washington selected Pierre L'Enfant to prepare the overall design for the new city. Trained as an architect in France, he had first come to the colonies in 1777, as part of a company of French volunteers with the Marquis de Lafayette, to serve in the Continental Army in the American war of independence. L'Enfant served in the corps of engineers and eventually attained the rank of major. Although L'Enfant's inspired plan proved to be an enduring framework for the new Federal City, he worked only briefly as an urban planner, being dismissed in 1792 after repeated conflicts with government officials.

At the core of L'Enfant's visionary plan was a new "Federal House," or what we know today as the Capitol. In a letter to George Washington, he recommended that this proposed legislative building be constructed on an elevated point above the Potomac River, at a spot called Jenkin's Hill, named after a farmer who leased land nearby. L'Enfant felt this choice acreage stood as a "pedestal waiting for a monument." Once this upland precinct was cleared of wood, he argued, it would be the logical home for the government of the United States of America.

L'Enfant's plan gained momentum in the 1790s when President George Washington, supported by his secretary of state, Thomas Jefferson, took the lead in eliciting plans for the new Capitol building. In a public competition, Washington called for architects to submit drawings for the proposed new government building. Sixteen men submitted plans, but none garnered any praise from Washington or his planners. The drawings were dismissed as either amateurish or uninspired, unworthy of the epochal undertaking at hand. One plan by James Diamond, an Irishman, called for an odd two-story structure with a huge rooster mounted atop its dome.

Finally, three months after the deadline had passed, a physician from the Virgin Islands named William Thornton submitted a plan that caught President Washington's eye, a sketch of a future Capitol building that embodied a sense of "grandeur" with the values of "simplicity" and "beauty." Thornton called for a domed structure with classical lines, reminiscent of the Pantheon

(LEFT)

BRUMIDI'S *APOTHEOSIS OF WASHINGTON.*
The allegorical fresco The Apotheosis of Washington *by Constantino Brumidi towers over the Rotunda of the Capitol building. Art and statuary are employed throughout the Capitol complex to chronicle the saga of American history, memorializing national heroes and historical events that shaped the course of the American experience.*

(RIGHT)

THE STATUE OF FREEDOM.
The bronze Statue of Freedom by Thomas Crawford stands majestically above the Capitol dome with a full moon as backdrop.

in Rome. President Washington himself participated in the laying of the cornerstone on September 18, 1793.

Legislators did not take up residence in the new "Federal House" until 1800, when President John Adams presided over a joint session of Congress. For many decades, the Capitol building was the temporary home of the Library of Congress, the Supreme Court, the federal district courts, and other government offices. In time, this initial structure was followed by the construction of the first separate buildings for the House of Representatives and the Senate. Overall, Capitol Hill in those formative years was a rather rustic place, surrounded by rolling hills and farmland.

If Goethe, the German writer, was correct in saying "architecture is frozen music," then the Capitol could be described as music with many composers. Today the impressive Capitol complex reflects, at a minimum, five distinct eras of construction from the 1790s to the 1960s—each phase defined by the shifting architectural whims of Congress. Architects Benjamin Henry Latrobe and Charles Bulfinch played major roles in the early decades, overseeing the baseline construction of the bicameral structure.

Latrobe, a favorite of Thomas Jefferson, oversaw the completion of separate House and Senate chambers, in the early days linked together only by a wooden walkway. He also modified the classical columns with capitals adorned with tobacco-leaf, corn-cob, and indigenous maize motifs, among many other creative touches. Assuming his architectural work in the years after the burning of the Capitol by the British in 1814, Boston architect Bulfinch oversaw the completion of the center section of the complex with a 55-foot-high dome in 1827. Bulfinch also was attentive to the general appearance of Capitol Hill, adding terraces, steps, gatehouses, and general landscaping.

The massive dome of the modern-day Capitol represents a dramatic departure from the low-lying wooden dome fashioned by Bulfinch. The change occurred during the tenure of Philadelphia architect Thomas U. Walter, who outlined a visionary expansion of the Capitol complex in the 1850s. His design work, in particular the call for a new and enlarged dome, continued through the years of the Civil War (1861–1865). Walter's design for the new dome called for the use of two cast-iron trussed shells,

THE PRESIDENT'S ROOM.
The ornate and lavish interior of the President's Room is filled with Italian frescoes by artist Constantino Brumidi and furniture characteristic of the 1870s. Completed in 1859, the room was originally used to sign legislation into law at the close of each congressional session. Today, the room is used by senators during interviews and press conferences.

CAPITOL HALLWAY.
As part of the Speaker's Lobby located behind the House of Representatives chamber, this hallway is used to exhibit portraits of every speaker of the House of Representatives since 1910. The collection also exhibits some portraits dating back to the eighteenth century, including Frederick A. C. Muhlenberg's portrait in 1789.

one superimposed on the other. Some critics in the nineteenth century considered the enlarged dome too massive and out of proportion. Yet, today, the distinctive dome appears to most observers to be in perfect harmony with its surroundings, an enduring and universal symbol of American democracy.

Atop the national Capitol is Thomas Crawford's bronze *Statue of Freedom*, a female figure of Freedom garbed in a flowing gown. Her right hand rests on a sheathed sword with her left holding a laurel wreath of victory and the shield of the United States with thirteen stripes. Her Roman-style helmet displays a circle of stars and a crest adorned with an eagle's head, feathers, and talons, a mirror of the distinctive costume of Native Americans. She stands on a cast-iron globe encircled with the national motto, *E Pluribus Unum*, and decorated at the base with fasces and wreaths. The bronze statue stands 19 feet 6 inches tall and weighs approximately 15,000 pounds. Her crest rises 288 feet above the east front plaza.

In 1863, even as the Civil War raged, the statue was installed on the dome, hoisted in sections and assembled atop the cast-iron pedestal. The final section, the figure's head

and shoulders, was raised on December 2, 1863, accompanied by a 35-gun salute, answered by the guns of the 12 forts around Washington. After nearly 130 years in place, the statue was detached from its pedestal and flown by helicopter to a special shop for restoration at the end of the twentieth century. Congress moved to conserve the famous bronze statue because of severe pitting and corrosion, cracks, and rusting on the cast-iron pedestal. The statue was returned by helicopter to its familiar place atop the Capitol in January 1993.

The splendid Rotunda beneath the cast-iron dome of the Capitol showcases Constantino Brumidi's fresco, *The Apotheosis of Washington*, and a frieze depicting triumphal moments in the American experience. Major themes of American history are projected onto canvas: the landing of Columbus, the embarkation of the Pilgrims, the Declaration of Independence, and the surrender of Cornwallis, among others. The lavish use of paintings, busts, statues, murals, and friezes employs art as a medium to capture a vivid image of American history. Nearby, the National Statuary Hall memorializes prominent figures, nominated by the various states for their significant impact on history.

CAPITOL HIDEAWAY.
Known as the "John F. Kennedy Room," this room was given to Senator Kennedy by the democratic leadership to use between his election in 1960 and his inauguration in 1961.

THE OLD SENATE CHAMBER.
Used by the Senate from 1810 to 1859, the Old Senate Chamber was once the sight of fierce debates between Daniel Webster, Henry Clay, and John C. Calhoun over issues such as slavery, territorial expansion, and economic policy. Later used by the Supreme Court, this room reflects the architectural efforts of Benjamin Henry Latrobe and Charles Bulfinch.

THE LIBRARY OF CONGRESS READING ROOM.
Congress purchased the private library of Thomas Jefferson to inaugurate the extraordinary book holdings of the Library of Congress. The library has grown over the years to become the largest in the world, occupying more than 530 miles of bookshelves.

ABRAHAM LINCOLN ARTIFACTS.
The Library of Congress exhibits the death mask of Abraham Lincoln and items in his pockets at the time of his assassination on April 14, 1865.

Near the Capitol is the monumental Library of Congress complex, housing the largest library in the world—the modern incarnation of a library that began when Congress purchased Thomas Jefferson's private library in 1800. The original building reflects the influence of the Beaux-Arts style at the turn of the twentieth century. The interior of the building, with its marble stairs, stained glass, vivid color, statuary, and cavernous reading room, evokes stunning beauty and remains a unique part of the Capitol complex.

Another nearby monumental architecture, combining classical motifs with elaborate detailing, is Union Station. Designed by Daniel H. Burnham, Union Station was built in 1908 adjacent to the Capitol, a spin-off of the McMillan Commission's ambitious plan to redesign the Mall. There had been a proposal to build a railroad aqueduct across the Mall, which at the turn of the twentieth century was the locale for a noisy and dirty stop on the Pennsylvania Railroad. Burnham played a key role in persuading the railroad president, A. J. Cassatt, to relocate in his grandiose neo-classical train station. Built in white marble with large Ionic columns, Union Station quickly rivaled Penn Station in New York City as one of America's most familiar public spaces. After decades of neglect, with leaking roofs and misuse, Union Station was renovated and reopened in 1988 and now occupies a lively space in the shadow of the Capitol with shops, restaurants, and railway links to America's cities and hinterlands.

The 1930s became a time of renewal for the Capitol complex. During this era of brick and mortar several important structures joined the ensemble: the U.S. Botanic Garden Conservatory and Bartholdi Park, among others. Nearby, the Library of Congress Annex, now named the John Adams Building, opened in 1939. A more austere edifice, the James Madison Building, became the third and final member of the Library of Congress complex in 1980.

In 1935, the stately Supreme Court building, with its classical lines, white façade and pediments, and spacious entrance plaza, was completed. For the first time since the inception of the Federal City, the Supreme Court took occupancy of its own choice lot on Capitol Hill.

UNION STATION.
Even in the air travel age, Union Station remains a vital and busy transportation link between Washington and other cities on the eastern seaboard. At one time or another, the station has housed a bowling alley, mortuary, bakery, butcher shop, YMCA, hotel, icehouse, liquor store, Turkish baths, and first-class restaurants. The stunning floodlit fountain at the renovated Union Station provides a grand entrance to one of the most visited sites in Washington.

(RIGHT)

THE BOTANICAL GARDENS.
The glass-domed Botanical Gardens, located at the east end of the Mall, houses an extraordinary collection of plants, even full-size trees.

(OPPOSITE)

THE BARTHOLDI FOUNTAIN.
The Bartholdi Fountain at the foot of Capitol Hill across from the Botanical Gardens was designed by Frederic Auguste Bartholdi for the Centennial of the United States in 1876.

(ABOVE)
PEDIMENT ON THE SUPREME COURT BUILDING. *Detail of the United States Supreme Court building, proclaiming "Equal justice under law." The pediment portrays the theme of "Liberty Enthroned Guarded by Order and Authority."*

(RIGHT)
SUPREME COURT PLAZA. *Supreme Court plaza with a bronze flagpole base in the foreground. Architect Cass Gilbert, Jr., designed the magnificent Supreme Court building in the classical style. The white marble structure was completed in 1935. Before this time, the Supreme Court was housed in numerous rooms in the Capitol until 1929, when former president and chief justice William Howard Taft persuaded Congress to construct a permanent home for the Court.*

(OPPOSITE)
SUPREME COURT ENTRANCE. *The shining bronze doors, sculpted by John Donnelly, Jr., provide an impressive entrance to the Supreme Court building. Each of the doors weighs six and one-half tons and depicts historic scenes in the development of law.*

(OPPOSITE AND ABOVE)
**OFFICES AND CHAMBERS
OF THE SUPREME COURT.**
*The chambers of Supreme Court
justices David Souter* (OPPOSITE)
and Ruth Ginsburg (ABOVE). *The
offices of the Supreme Court
justices convey a sense of
authority and dignity with
wood-paneled walls, books,
and comfortable leather chairs.*

(RIGHT)
**SUPREME COURT
LIBRARY.**
*The Supreme Court building
maintains its own research
library. The library serves as
an essential resource in the
work of the highest court
in the land.*

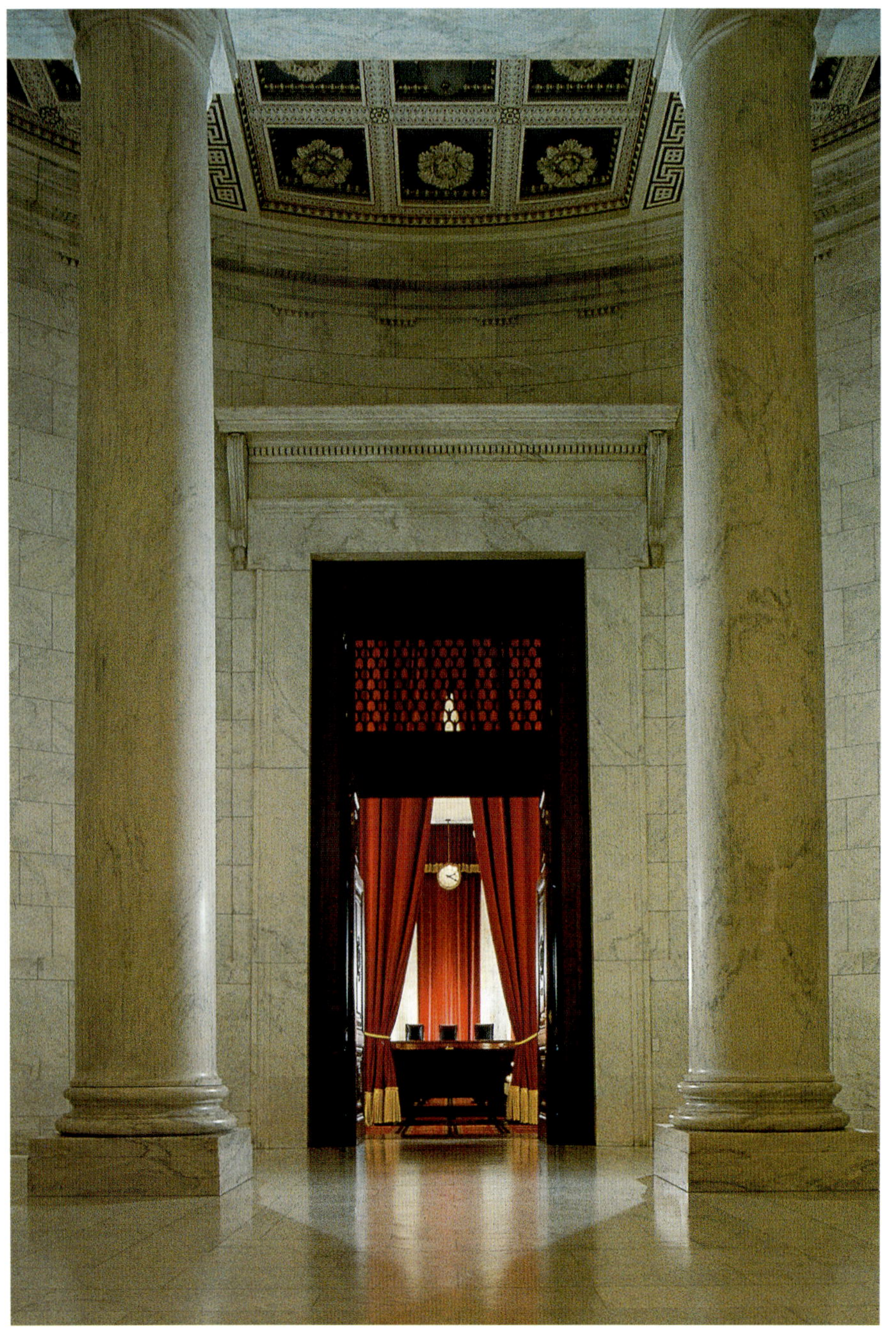

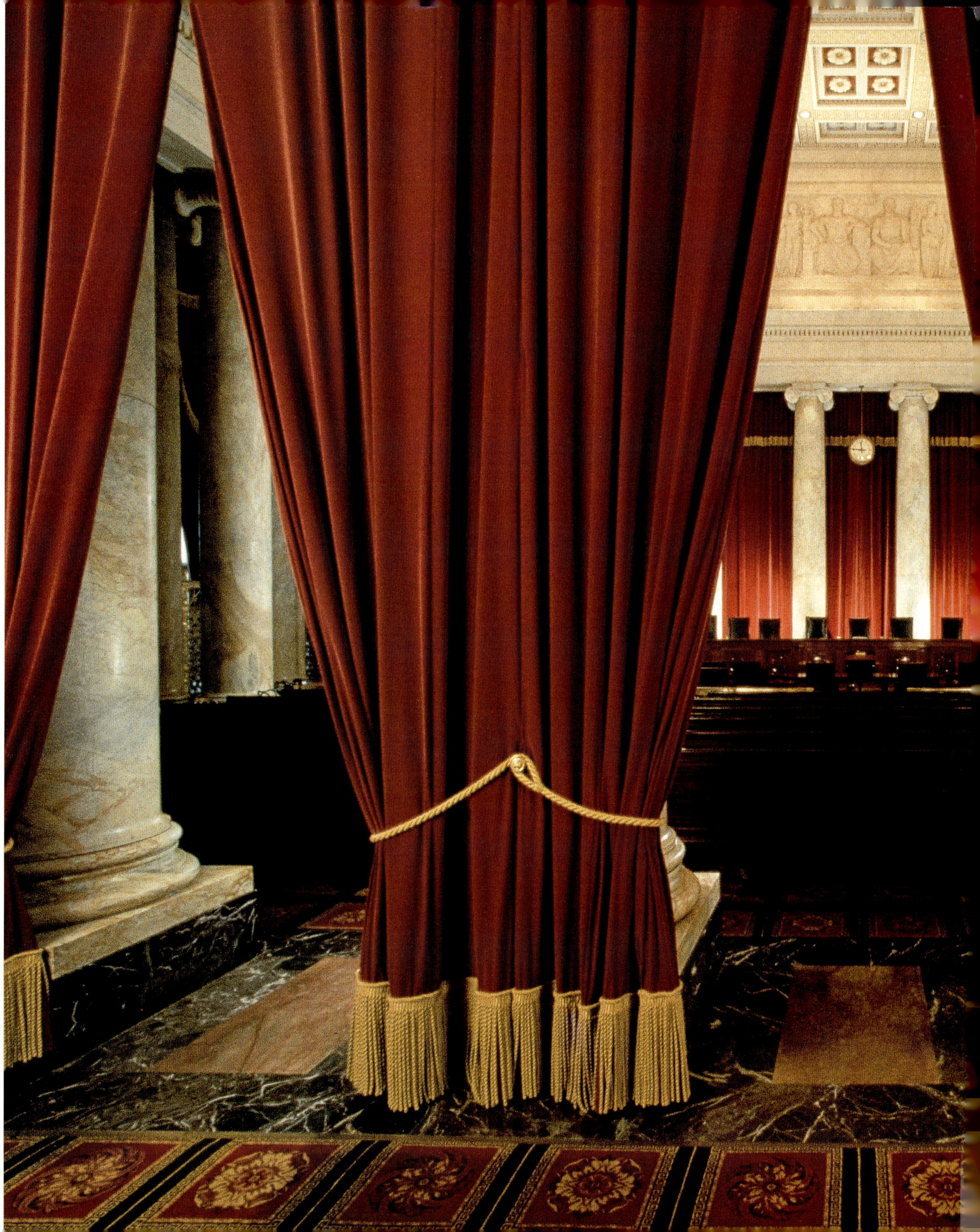

(ABOVE)
ENTRANCE TO THE SUPREME COURTROOM.
The entrance into the Courtroom, from the Great Hall. Behind the marble columns in the Great Hall are busts of all former chief justices.

(ABOVE)
VIEW OF THE SUPREME COURTROOM FROM THE BENCH.

The bench of the Supreme Court provides a breathtaking view of the Courtroom. Seating on the bench is determined by seniority. The chief justice sits in the center, the senior associate justice to the immediate right, and the two most junior justices at either end.

(LEFT)
VIEW OF THE SUPREME COURT BENCH.

A view from the back of the Courtroom looking toward the bench. When Cass Gilbert designed this room, he wanted it to stand out as the focal point of the building, thus he enlisted the aid of Benito Mussolini to assist him in acquiring the best quality Italian marble. In thanking Mussolini for his help with the acquisition, Gilbert sent his "most cordial wishes for your health and the prosperity of your great regime and the glory of Italy." *After the building's completion, light from the adjacent courtyards made the room extremely bright, so heavy draperies were added to mask the light. The draperies also helped to improve the poor acoustics, inherent in Gilbert's original design.*

(PAGE 132)
THE WEST PORTICO OF THE SUPREME COURT BUILDING.

A passerby views the columns of the West Portico of the Supreme Court. The Supreme Court convenes in October and hears oral arguments for cases it has consented to review. Decisions of this last court of appeal are typically announced in May or June of each year.